BOOST YOUR
CONFIDENCE
WITH NLP

Other books by Ian McDermott

The Coaching Bible (with Wendy Jago)
The NLP Coach (with Wendy Jago)
Your Inner Coach (with Wendy Jago)
Way of NLP (with Joseph O'Connor)
First Directions NLP (with Joseph O'Connor)
Manage Yourself, Manage Your Life (with Ian Shircore)
Practical NLP for Managers (with Joseph O'Connor)
NLP and the New Manager (with Ian Shircore)
NLP and Health (with Joseph O'Connor)
Brief NLP Therapy (with Wendy Jago)
The Art of Systems Thinking (with Joseph O'Connor)
Develop Your Leadership Qualities (with Joseph O'Connor et al)
Take Control of Your Life (with Joseph O'Connor et al)

Coaching CDs by Ian McDermott

Essential Coaching Skills
How to Coach Yourself
The Spiritual Dimension of Coaching
Freedom from the Past
Tools for Transformation
An Introduction to NLP: Psychological Skills for Understanding and Handling People
(with Joseph O'Connor)
The Power to Change
Professional Development Programme

BOOST YOUR CONFIDENCE WITH NLP

SIMPLE TECHNIQUES FOR A MORE CONFIDENT AND SUCCESSFUL YOU

IAN McDERMOTT

piatkus

PIATKUS

First published in Great Britain in 2010 by Piatkus
Reprinted 2012

Copyright © 2010 by Ian McDermott

A CIP catalogue record for this book
is available from the British Library.

ISBN 978-0-7499-2851-3

Typeset in Stone Serif by M Rules
Printed and bound by CPI Group (UK) Ltd, Croydon, CR0 4YY

Papers used by Piatkus are from well-managed forests
and other responsible sources.

MIX
Paper from
responsible sources
FSC® C104740

Piatkus
An imprint of
Little, Brown Book Group
100 Victoria Embankment
London EC4Y 0DY

An Hachette UK Company
www.hachette.co.uk

www.piatkus.co.uk

For Paulette
who had the confidence
to trust her heart

Contents

Acknowledgements

This book wouldn't exist if it were not for the prompting of Gill Bailey who convinced me I really should get round to writing it. For nigh on thirty years Gill has commissioned and then offered sage input to a whole generation of authors. I count myself lucky to have been one of them for the past decade. I wish her well in her new supposedly more relaxed role as Consultant Editor.

Thanks too to the outstanding Piatkus team, especially Rebecca Woods and Karen Ings for their encouragement, care and attention to detail. It's been a pleasure working with you.

And of course special thanks to my Skype companion Susan Clark without whom this book might never have come to fruition.

The field of NLP wouldn't exist if it were not for the innovative creativity first of its founders Richard Bandler and John Grinder and then of my NLP friends and colleagues who have contributed so much to the exploration of excellence since the late 1970s. My thanks to them all for their contributions, which this book naturally draws on, but also for the joy of working and creating together. Thanks also to my clients and students who frequently stimulated me to develop some of the tools you are about to start using.

Finally – and always – there is my wife Paulette who has to live with a man with a mission. As ever, thank you for supporting me that I may support others.

About the Author

Ian McDermott is the man who brought NLP and Coaching together. The world's foremost authority on NLP Coaching, he is the bestselling author of The NLP Coach and the author of the chapter on NLP Coaching in the industry-standard manual Excellence in Coaching.

Ian is the founder of International Teaching Seminars (ITS), which celebrated its twentieth anniversary in 2008. ITS is a world leader in delivering NLP training and coaching and the primary resource for more than a hundred of the world's top companies and organisations. Clients range right across the private and public sectors, including charities and NGOs.

A visionary entrepreneurial leader, Ian spends much of his time training the next generation of executives, coaches and NLP practitioners. Through ITS Executive Coaching, Ian and an elite group of specialists focus on strategic issues, creativity and innovation. His work is featured in the Open University's MBA course 'Creativity, Innovation and Change'.

Named one of Britain's Top 10 Coaches and described as 'the Coaches' Coach' (*Independent*), Ian continues to work with individuals who want to make change happen. A UKCP-registered psychotherapist and a longstanding member of the Society of Authors, he is the co-author of some of the most widely read and respected books in the field, including: *Way of NLP*; *Practical NLP for Managers*; *NLP and Health*; *The Art of Systems Thinking*; *NLP and the New Manager*; *Manage Yourself, Manage Your Life*; *Brief NLP Therapy*; *The NLP Coach*; *Your Inner Coach*; and *The Coaching Bible*. His books have been translated into fifteen languages.

Ian is also the founder of the Confidence Institute.

Introduction

Experience tells you what to do; confidence allows you to do it.

Stan Smith, tennis professional

Just as I was sitting down to write this introduction, the phone rang. It was a client of mine, the director of a large UK government research institute. In the course of our conversation, he told me about a meeting in Whitehall he'd just attended where he'd proposed that a new structure be created which would have ultimately put him and a number of directors out of a job. The mandarins had looked horrified, but as my client said: 'That didn't scare me, because I'm confident I could always find another position – and that's down to the NLP skills I've acquired.'

So often people hold back because they're afraid – afraid of failing or looking foolish, afraid of being rejected, or afraid of losing what they hold dear, be it a job, a relationship or just a familiar routine. Confidence enables you to step up to the plate and *live*. That's why it's so important. It's not an optional extra or the icing on the cake. It's more like the magic ingredient which holds everything together. And when it's not there, in extreme cases, that's when you hear people say they feel like they're falling apart.

Confidence is more than a mood; it's a way of thinking. Ultimately, confident living is a way of being. In this book we're going to cover all three aspects – how to *feel confident*, learning the skill of *thinking confidently*, and being able to *live confidently*.

When I first began to pay attention to the whole idea of confidence in our everyday lives, what really struck me was that no other single human concept I can think of – none – has more influence over all our lives, each and every day. There are no human interactions, either with others or even with ourselves, where confidence, in some shape or form, is not playing a part.

Take an everyday, even humdrum, experience; you decide to go on a shopping trip and set off in full confidence that (a) your car will start and get you to the mall, (b) the shops will be open, (c) your credit card will not be declined because (d) your employer has paid your wages this month. Each of these assumptions is an indicator of what you can reasonably assume to be the case. Most people don't give these factors a second thought because they are confident they can rely on the world to work this way.

Take a more profound experience: you and your partner decide to have a baby because you are confident that (a) you can, (b) you have what it takes to learn to be good parents, (c) the pregnancy itself will not be life-threatening, (d) you will produce a healthy child, (e) your child will survive into adulthood, and (f) parenting must be rewarding or surely people would only do it once and never again! That's a lot to assume! Some of what you're taking for granted – (c), (d) and (e) – would have seemed absolutely mad to any human being who ever lived before, say, 1900. So the assumptions we make tell us a lot about the confidence we have in the world we inhabit and the way it works.

Confidence is the crucial glue or currency in every single human action, interaction and undertaking that I can think of. It is not just something you need if you're dating – though it helps! Like I said, it is *not* an optional extra. This is what drove me to set up the Confidence Institute, which is dedicated to the promotion of confidence as a learnable skill.

To help you grasp the lie of the land, let me explain how this book is organised. There are three parts. In Part 1, Building Confidence, I want to make clear what the payoffs of boosting your confidence will be for you specifically. In Chapter 1, I will introduce you to some of the best-kept secrets of the study of human behaviour, otherwise known as Neuro-linguistic Programming (NLP). In Chapter 2, we'll start to focus on the different types of confidence and find out which tools are going to be most useful for you to develop. This will make it much easier for you to get results. We'll also address how much confidence is enough and how much is too much. Being overconfident can breed complacency and arrogance – and this can have dire consequences, as we saw in the global financial meltdown that started in 2008. In Chapter 3, we're going to use the Confidence Balance Wheel to test your confidence right now and figure out how you can get major enhancements in confidence in one area of your life by taking care of business in another.

In Part 2, Applied Confidence, I want to show you how to develop what I call '4×4 confidence'. A 4-wheel-drive vehicle gives you the ability to handle most terrains and in all weathers. Wouldn't it be nice if you could handle the rugged terrain of life with the same kind of robust versatility? To do so you need to know about the Four Pillars of Confidence and the Four Keys to Confidence. These will help you step out of your current comfort zone and safely face any and all challenges. That's what we'll be doing in Chapter 4.

In Chapters 5 and 6, I will give you specific NLP techniques to build confidence in relationships and your professional life respectively. Then, in Chapter 7, I focus on confidence, health and wealth and how they interact. In a very real sense your health *is* your wealth. You have the power to do something about both – and I will be showing you how.

Part 3, Living with Confidence, takes all the issues we've covered so far, including all the 'how to' techniques, and looks at them in the larger context of a life well lived – both what that means to you and what it's going to take to achieve it. Everybody's life has ups and downs, so if you're going to live with confidence then, paradoxically, you need to know what to do if and when confidence deserts you. Chapter 8 will give you the tools and techniques you – and those you care about – will need during such times.

Having some understanding of your life journey is also a crucial part of living with confidence. Chapter 9 is dedicated to what is known as 'The Hero's Journey', where the hero is – you! Finally, living with confidence invariably involves being able to see beyond our own little world and having the ability to play a bigger game. This is often what makes life truly fulfilling. And those who are fulfilled are always confident. That's why Chapter 10 explores Confidence in the Bigger Picture. I want to finish by exploring with you what such fulfilment – and consequently confidence – might mean for you.

As with any new skill, building confidence is going to take practice. You are not going to finish reading this book and suddenly wake up the next morning bathed in a new and mystical everlasting glow of confidence. To boost your own confidence levels, and to make them last, you're going to need to work your way through the exercises I have included throughout the book. Some of these are techniques which have been developed over the years by myself and my colleagues, others I have created to meet the needs of clients I've been working with. All have one thing in common. They are examples of NLP in action because they offer a step by step approach which is derived from observing best practice in those demonstrating it. As we'll be seeing later, NLP is about modeling excellence, i.e. looking for what works and then figuring out what it is that a person or an organisiation actually does that makes them outstanding. When we've figured this out we can test our hypotheses and if they stand up we will then have something that we can teach other people who want to improve their performance in the same field.

That's why doing the exercises is worth your while. They are tried and tested and you'll be much better prepared for whatever comes your way in the future. Indeed, one way you can think of confidence is as a kind of inoculation against trouble. The more confident you are, the more you can handle yourself. The more confident you are, the more you can actually be who you really are. That's good for you and it's good for the world.

It's also what has inspired me to spend the last thirty years working with people. In that time I have seen many people grow into their confidence and become who they really could be. If you want to know more about my background, see About the Author on page xi. For now, though, I think a few headlines will be enough, as I'm keen to get started.

Over twenty years ago I founded International Teaching Seminars (ITS), an organisation that has been extraordinarily successful in pioneering the *practical* application of NLP to numerous areas of personal and organisational development. Then I brought NLP and coaching together – see my book *The NLP Coach* – to create the best of both worlds. This created an explosion of interest. Much of my time since then has been devoted to training the next generation of practitioners and advising large organisations on how to implement these amazing ways of working. Now I'd like to share them with you.

Ian McDermott, 2010

PART I

BUILDING CONFIDENCE

Chapter 1

The Fruits of Confidence

Grow Your Own

Not so long ago, an American model launched a new perfume called Chosen. It was, she said, the first ever fragrance to capture the 'scent' of confidence and the women who wore it would feel they, like her, had been *'chosen to walk in confidence'*. For less than $20, a woman could obtain all the confidence she needed to face the world. Confidence captured in a chic little bottle: all she would need to do is squirt and go. In the same way, with his branded cologne for men called Instinct, it is the fruits of confidence that football icon David Beckham is harnessing. The marketing campaign promised that the scent would give a man the *'confidence of his masculinity'*.

Confidence, then, would seem to be a pretty desirable commodity for both men and women. But trying to spray it on probably won't deliver what you're looking for. That's because confidence comes from the inside.

In this book I want to show you how you can build confidence in easy, manageable stages – be it in yourself or others. I also want to introduce to you to the different dimensions of confidence so you can customise what we do. Plus I want to give you a whole raft of specific tools which will make it possible for you to move forward easily and, dare I say it, with confidence.

But before we get into any of this I want to make clear to you exactly why I believe confidence is so important in both our personal and professional lives.

I can best do this by looking at what happens when confidence is missing. A lack of confidence makes us feel shaky. And this is true whether it's lack of confidence in ourselves or in others. If you feel shaky, it's hard to engage and commit and go for what you want – and this holds true whether it's committing emotionally to a relationship or financially to a new business opportunity.

Ultimately, though, confidence is not about being able to live the life of some celebrity extrovert; it's about being able to live fully and freely as *yourself*.

Confidence – The Real Benefits

Increased confidence can produce truly profound changes. I have been working with clients – both corporate and individual – for thirty years and I have seen these changes at first hand. As I was gathering the material together to write this book, I decided to make a list of the most important changes I'd witnessed over the years. Putting all these positive experiences together surprised even me. It's what made me found the Confidence Institute. I think you'll agree it really is remarkable just how much confidence can deliver.

Put it this way: suppose you were offered a product that had the following payoffs, would you be interested?

- You can be yourself, rather than trying to be who you think others expect you to be.
- You don't have to pretend to agree with others when you don't agree at all.
- You can handle challenges.
- You're not afraid to challenge yourself.
- You no longer live in fear of being 'found out' or found wanting.
- You can stop worrying about losing face.
- You can live with uncertainty.
- You don't have to pretend you have all the answers.
- You can handle the unexpected.
- You can stop forever seeking approval.
- You can be more inquiring because you won't be afraid to ask questions and show you don't always know the answers.
- You will be more playful and less serious.
- You'll likely be more optimistic.
- You'll be healthier; psychoneuroimmunology studies prove your immune system is directly affected by your confidence levels.
- You'll be more resilient when the going gets tough.
- You'll be better able to handle yourself and others making mistakes.
- You'll be able to forgive yourself and others.
- You'll also come across as more human because you don't need to be perfect.

And as if that wasn't enough, consider this: only when you are confident can you commit *wholeheartedly* to anything.

Of course, your confidence levels don't just affect you; they can influence and even change how *other* people think, feel and perform. There is, if you will, a currency of confidence which we all trade in everyday. As with any other currency, the exchange rate can vary day by day. It all depends on how we come across and how others perceive us.

Why NLP Is the Best Tool for Building Confidence

If you want to boost confidence, NLP is going to be very useful to you because it can deliver practical tools and intensively tested techniques that deliver results. So what is it? NLP stands for Neuro (N) Linguistic (L) Programming (P). And what, you may ask, is that?

Neuro: The mind-body relationship and how it works.

Linguistic: The language we use to describe and make sense of our world.

Programming: Repeating patterns of thought and behaviour that help or hinder us.

As the name suggests, it's a synthesis of different disciplines. The way we use our mind and body affects our behaviour and produces repeated patterns that run like computer programs in our life – for good or ill. NLP looks at how we do this. It's interested in the mechanics of our experience because when you understand how you do something, you have the power to either change or improve it. So if you knew *how* you made yourself feel on top form (or terrible), you'd be able to improve your mood; if you knew what *exactly* you did that got you the job, you'd be able to repeat it in future; but equally if you knew *how* someone else finds it easy to remember people's names, you could learn how to do this too; if you knew how someone else had come through adversity, you could learn how to do the same.

One of the real contributions NLP can make is to answer the question: how do you *do* that? And it can give you the tools and techniques to find this out for yourself. NLP then is about learning the 'how to's so that what one person can do, others can learn to do too. This applies to learning how to be more confident in just the same way as it applies to being able to remember people's names.

NLP is often formally defined as 'the study of the *structure* of subjective experience'. So if I am working with someone who is not very confident, I want to know *how* they do not being very confident. If, as with one client, you imagine going to meet people and in your head you run a movie of them turning their backs on you and if, as you run that movie, you also have a soundtrack of your own voice saying 'You'll never be any good at this', you have a very effective structure for undermining your own confidence! The structure is the movie and the soundtrack. If we change the content of what's going on in that movie and what you are saying to yourself on the soundtrack, you will have a totally different experience. The structure – i.e. movie + sound-track – has stayed the same, but the content is very different.

For most of its history, NLP has also distinguished itself by looking for what works and by seeking out models of excellence. For this reason, the other formal definition of NLP is 'the study of excellence'. So if you want to know how to be more confident, NLP would suggest you don't spend your time studying people who aren't confident. There are a thousand ways not to be confident. Instead, find people who are confident either because they 'naturally' are that way or because they have learnt how to be. Either way, what we want to ask each one of them is: *how do you do that?* That's the NLP question. We want to know the 'how to's of confidence. And that's what the rest of this book is about.

As part of making sense of our world, we create what, in NLP, we call models of reality. Spend time with a child and you can see this process happening in front of your eyes as they try to make sense of the world. We keep doing this throughout our lives: you have an experience and you draw conclusions from it. One client who had been betrayed by her adolescent love drew the conclusion that all men are bastards. That was the model she operated out of from then on – and was surprised to find that the men she

chose really were bastards! The reason these models are so important is that we go on to operate in the world *as if* our models are
true. The model you have of how things work can either
strengthen or undermine your confidence.

* * * * *

NLP was born in the 1970s. We've been studying people and
organisations who are models of excellence ever since. Invariably
what has been discovered has then been formatted into learnable
strategies and techniques that can be taught to anyone who
wants to learn how to excel. I have found some of these techniques to be particularly effective in boosting confidence, so I
want to show you how to learn and apply them.

But before we go much further, I want to ask you a fundamental NLP question: what do you really want out of this book? Being
clear about your outcome is fundamental to success. One of the
distinguishing features of people who achieve their goals is that
they actually know what their goals are! That means they know
what the goal will look like, sound like and feel like when they
achieve what they're going for. They can imagine it now and this
helps their brain steer a course in the desired direction. Putting a
time frame on this is also something that achievers invariably do.
Without a stated outcome, you are much more likely to be blown
off course by external events. So take a minute and just get clear
about the confidence journey you want to make.

EXERCISE: Setting Your Goals

Finish the sentences below to clarify what you want and how
you'll know when you've got it.

I'm reading this book because . . . .
So my outcome is to . . . .

I'll know when I've achieved this because I will

see ....

hear ....

feel ....

By the end of this book, I want to ....

....

Just by becoming more curious about yourself and by starting to pay more attention to the consequences and effects of what you do, you will begin to get a better sense of what works (and indeed what you need to ditch). By doing this you can start to play to your strengths. It's NLP in action and anyone can do it. As you hone this skill, you can begin to apply it to building confidence. Use all of your senses – seeing, hearing, feeling, smelling and tasting – to get this information. I'll show you how as we progress through the book.

You will almost certainly find it useful to be able to examine the world from a number of different perspectives. I'll give you a specific technique so you can learn this as a skill. Confident people don't need to be dogmatic; they can see different points of view. The more flexible you can be when examining a situation, the more information you will be able to gather and the more choices you will discover. The greatest thing about having more choice is that it automatically confers more confidence. Just how confident do you feel when you're boxed in and there's only one option?

My advice is to always give yourself three options or choices and know what your preferred outcome really is. That way the behaviour you choose can serve your outcome. Human behaviour is always a means to an end. So on any given occasion it's really useful to know what you're going for. Knowing that you are more than your behaviour is going to make a big difference to your confidence levels. That's why later on we're going to spend a bit of time getting to know you in such a way that you have a deeper and clearer relationship with yourself. After all, if you're not confident in the relationship you have with yourself, how can you expect to be confident in relationships with others?

Getting Real about Confidence

Nobody – and I mean nobody – is confident all the time, in all situations. You may be more (or less) confident in some areas of your life, you may be more (or less) confident in certain settings and you may feel more (or less) confident on any given day. And that's just you on your own! On any given day, other people will have more or less confidence in themselves, in you and your abilities and you in theirs. This is the currency of confidence; these are the endlessly shifting confidence exchange rates.

You know how your opinion about a co-worker can change depending on how competently you feel they handled a recent challenge? You may have more or less confidence in their abilities than before – or they in you for that matter. The same is true nationally and internationally. Just remember the widespread insecurity resulting from the global loss of confidence in financial institutions in 2008–9. This produced a fundamental loss of business confidence and ordinary people paid the price.

When such things happen people are very aware that they're living in turbulent times, but in truth the loss of confidence is never just in the economy. A lot of that turbulence is to be found inside *us*, because people experience heightened levels of stress, worry and anxiety. In such times personal confidence becomes all the more precious.

For most people, confidence is a feeling. If you have it, you can move mountains. If you don't, you're more likely to become dispirited. But confidence is also a way of thinking. How you think about the challenges facing you will affect how you feel about them. That's why we're going to spend some time learning how to think differently.

If you're interested in boosting your confidence, your thoughts are going to be as significant as your feelings. Belief in yourself is profoundly affected by how you think about yourself. Noticing the kind of thoughts you have and whether or not they boost your confidence will therefore be important. Take, for instance, your internal dialogue – just how do you talk to yourself on the inside? Do you encourage yourself and review realistically, or do you criticise, disparage and carp at yourself? And just what sort of tone of voice do you use? That tone can make you feel wretched or supported.

Whether it's a sense of sureness in yourself or in others, confidence plays a pivotal role in how we interact and communicate with each other. This holds true whether you're a major financial institution or a private individual. Confidence gives us a sense there is something concrete and stable we can rely on, which in turn gives us a reality we can trust.

What confidence can do is improve your ability to handle the unexpected. To maintain confidence when all around you appear to be collapsing is not easy, but it is possible. The secret is to understand that confidence has nothing to do with control. You know there are huge global forces you cannot control. Likewise, in our personal lives, there are those who we may wish to change but in truth can never control. However, if you have confidence in yourself, you will not need to try to control the world or others and you can begin to shape your own world.

When we're in transition we're often less confident, because the old ways no longer suffice but the new ways are not yet in place or familiar. If you've ever changed career or become self-employed, you'll know what I'm talking about. This is part of what's going on with teenagers, too – they don't want to be treated as children but they don't want the full burden of adult responsibility, either. A similar thing can happen with corporations in transition or who are reinventing themselves – there can be uncertainty and unsureness and a loss of the old confidence.

So confidence is a constantly fluctuating state. I find that if I'm going to work with a person, a team or a corporation, it's useful to know what triggers these fluctuations. So I'll often ask them what would undermine confidence around here and what would really lift it?

Sometimes it's really obvious. Suppose you knew someone who woke up this morning to discover they'd lost their job, their partner had walked out and their doctor called to say test results confirmed they had a serious illness. You wouldn't exactly be surprised if their confidence had taken a nosedive.

At the macro level the same holds true: external events like world economic recession can trigger a sudden and devastating loss of confidence both individually and collectively. So your confidence level is not just about you, it's also related to the changing circumstances you are dealing with.

* * * * *

As we start this journey, you may also want to ask yourself if there is anything that will further support you as you develop and hone your confidence skills. Are there particular people, activities, routines and rituals that will help you and how are you going to make sure those are in your life? Let me give you a personal example. I've been self-employed virtually my entire working life. I was aware from the outset that I would find this much easier if I enjoyed good health and had plenty of energy. So I do a whole bunch of things that improve my health and well-being. For instance, for over twenty years I've had acupuncture once a fortnight because it really works for me. It strengthens me – and my confidence. Is there anything that does the same for you? Are you getting it when you need it?

Finally, a crucial aspect of getting real about confidence is the understanding that confidence shows up in very different ways –

maybe more ways than you've imagined. It takes confidence, for example, to ask for and accept guidance and to admit, comfortably, that you don't know everything. A journalist friend once told me the best technique she learned for dealing with editors, especially early on in her career, was never to feel defensive when they asked their supplementary questions about the stories she filed. She became adept at saying, 'I don't know, but I can find out.' And they loved her for it. In the same vein, a student of mine worked for the Royal Mail and told me of a training day he'd attended where, unusually, he'd been the oldest person in the room by a good twenty years. While the younger guys felt they had to pretend they already knew everything, he had the confidence to ask questions. They feared they'd be losing face, but he had a productive and enjoyable day bombarding the trainer with questions.

The United States of Confidence

Just as you can create greater self-confidence, so you can enable others to achieve this too. To *inspire* confidence in others is to leave a lasting impact. This can be a formidable legacy. Barack Obama's 2008 election campaign slogan of 'Yes we can' asserted faith in a people's ability to rise to the challenge. It contains something else too, a natural by-product of confidence – optimism.

Many studies are now showing high correlations between being optimistic and being healthy and living longer. Just one example: a 2004 Dutch study found that optimistic people live 29 per cent longer than pessimists!

In my experience, the United States is a can-do culture and naturally optimistic. I often find it useful to ask clients what kind of culture they're creating in their family and their workplace. How about yours? Does it support an optimistic outlook?

Confidence allows you to be optimistic, not because everything will be just fine but because you have reason to believe that you can rise to the challenge.

On her first European tour with her husband, Michelle Obama spoke to teenage schoolgirls in the UK. Afterwards they could not stop raving about how she had inspired them to want more, do more and aim for more. She told them that the world was counting on them to 'be the very best you can be'.

This is the gift of confidence. I'd like to begin to show how you and those you care for can be the best you can be.

Chapter 2

Types of Confidence

How We Talk about Confidence

Think about all the different ways we talk about confidence. You may, for example, decide to take one of your friends *into your confidence* over a private matter; you may give a work colleague your *vote of confidence*; you may divulge information in *strictest confidence*; you may fall out with a friend you feel has *betrayed your confidence*; you might even, if you are very unlucky and they are very good at *winning your confidence*, fall prey to a *confidence trickster*.

There are so many situations in which confidence is critical. So what is the formal definition of confidence, a word we use in so many different ways? According to the *Oxford English Dictionary*, it is 'firm trust, a feeling of reliance or certainty, a sense of self-reliance; boldness'. Linguistically, it stems from *fidere*, the Latin word meaning to trust, which is also the root of the word faith.

Confidence and trust, then, are natural bedfellows.

Read the following two statements aloud and ask yourself: which of these two people would you place your confidence in?

He had a loud confidence that spilled out everywhere, drowning out the doubts of others.

She had a quiet confidence that made people listen to her, trust her judgement and follow her advice.

Was it the loud confidence of someone who cannot even hear the opinions of others that attracted you, or the quiet, sure confidence of someone it feels like you can trust? Which wins your vote?

There really are different kinds of confidence, and as you start to boost your own confidence levels it's going to be important to identify what kind of confidence you need and which is the right kind for you. So let's get started. Jot down the names of five people in your life who you have confidence in. Then write one sentence saying why you trust them. It may be that you trust your partner with the family finances, or you trust your boss to make the right decision about choosing between two seemingly evenly matched supply companies. It may be that you trust your doctor to ensure you see the right specialist. Maybe you are confident that the neighbour who pops in to feed the cat is following your instructions and giving your pet the right amount of food on time.

It's going to be helpful for you to begin making some distinctions about the degree and the kind of confidence you have in a particular person and a particular context.

Whenever I do this with clients, they realise that you may have confidence in someone in one aspect of your relationship but not in another. For example, you may trust your partner with the family finances, but not with cooking Sunday lunch. Or you may trust your pet-sitter with your animal, but not with your partner!

EXERCISE: Different Kinds of Confidence

I have confidence in . . . . . to . . . . because . . . .

I have confidence in . . . . . to . . . . because . . . .

I have confidence in . . . . . to . . . . because . . . .

I have confidence in . . . . . to . . . . because . . . .

I have confidence in . . . . . to . . . . because . . . .

Now, turn this exercise on its head. Think of five people in your life in whom you have no confidence in a particular area.

I have no confidence in . . . . to . . . . . . because . . . .

I have no confidence in . . . . to . . . . . . because . . . .

I have no confidence in . . . . to . . . . . . because . . . .

I have no confidence in . . . . to . . . . . . because . . . .

I have no confidence in . . . . to . . . . . . because . . . .

Be as specific as you can: for example, I have no confidence in my teenager daughter to put the rubbish bins out for me when I am away next week because she forgot to do it the last time. I have no confidence in my wife to stay within our agreed budget this month because I know she is going shopping with her sister at the weekend and will allow herself to be talked into buying yet another pair of shoes.

Looking at the results of this exercise, notice how confidence – or the lack of it – occurs in a particular context: the mother who does not trust her daughter to take out the rubbish; the husband who does not trust his wife with their money.

Confidence does not exist alone or in isolation. There is always a context and a relationship. And just as this applies to our confidence levels in others, it also applies to our confidence in ourselves. You probably feel more confident in some settings than others. So it's going to be useful to take stock of where and when you have it – and where and when you need more of it.

Life as a One-man Band

An important part of finding out about your confidence, as it stands now, is to look at your confidence in the people around you, at work and at home.

Are you, for example, confident enough in others to delegate? If you can't delegate in the office, what does that tell you about your colleagues and about you? Do they need more training? Are you simply working in the wrong environment for you and with the wrong people? Or do you need to learn how to let go and trust? Similarly, if you know that you cannot delegate at home, ask yourself: why not? It's important to look at the confidence you place in other people, because if you don't – if you have no confidence in anyone but yourself – you will actually limit what you can achieve. You may see self-reliance as a good thing, but it can stop you being a good team player, an attitude which will impact adversely on your work and home life.

When you do have confidence in others and know you can trust your own judgement and rely on them, then you can successfully delegate and allow other people to play to their strengths. Having more confidence will allow you to be more innovative. In business terms it can give you the strength to take more risks, and go beyond the mindset of being an employee just following orders.

Of course it's also going to be useful to get a sense of how confident others are in you. Knowing that people have placed their confidence in you boosts your self-esteem. It means you have champions or allies who believe in you and in getting the best out of you. When I first started working out with a personal trainer, we would do our warm-up exercises and then run up a very long and steep hill next to my home. I hated this hill and dreaded having to find the energy and the will to push myself to keep going and get to the top of it. But my trainer, who knew this – and had the measure of me – would turn to me about halfway up and say, in the quiet but confident way he had about him: 'You can do this, Ian.' And I found that in fact he was right. This not only increased my confidence in him as a trainer, but also in my own judgement: the longer we worked together, the more apparent it was that I'd made the right choice when I was deciding who to hire.

Shyness and Confidence

Nigella Lawson, the British television chef, author and journalist, says she was a shy and timid child who dreaded it when her parents' friends visited because she would then have to converse with grown-ups, a prospect she found terrifying. So how has she ended up with a high-profile television career and a life lived under the often intense and critical scrutiny of the public eye?

'When I was first asked to present my own cookery programme, my first reaction was fear,' she says. 'But then the excitement kicked in. I made a concerted effort to go with the excited feeling, rather than the frightened one, because I knew I'd be [more] annoyed with myself if I said no to something because it was scary, than if I did it and failed.'

As someone who says that underneath her public exterior she is still a shy person, Nigella understands you have to work at confidence and find techniques that are effective for you: 'I've found, that for me, doing things at the last minute is a good practice when you're not confident.'

Being shy is just one way in which you may lack confidence. However, many people who lack confidence don't come across as shy.

If you lack confidence, there will be many self-imposed inhibitions you experience as you try to minimise your discomfort and protect yourself. You may be someone who lacks the confidence to speak their own truth and, as a result, suffers in silence. You may not be assertive and feel as if you have no voice of your own. You may not be confident around figures of authority, or you may simply be shy when socialising.

Feeling and being self-inhibited, in a thousand different ways, is the price you pay for lacking in confidence. You may sit through and then pay for a horrible cold meal in a restaurant because you are not confident enough to send it back to the kitchen; you may skip a meal rather than face eating alone when you are away on a business trip; you may skulk in your hotel room because you don't have the confidence to do things on your own. But none of these behaviours necessarily means that you're shy.

Confidence training can address any and all of these different inhibitions. It is akin to using a muscle you may never have realised you even had. That muscle is there, but it needs developing and it is this confidence muscle that this book will help you train and develop.

Overconfidence

Most people simply think of confidence as this wonderful attribute that is so desirable, we all want more of it, all the time. But this is not necessarily true. Think back to the impact of the recent global financial crisis and you have a textbook example of what happens when organisations and individuals have too much confidence. Yes, of course, more confidence *can* be a good thing, but not if it leads to overconfidence, because overconfidence leads to recklessness.

The collapse of the financial markets was a direct result of an irrational exuberance among those involved in the world of finance. They convinced themselves the impossible was possible – markets would just keep going up. This overconfidence flew in the face of all past history, which tells us this will not and cannot be the case.

Overconfidence can also lead to boredom. We tend to perform best when we are at the edge of our confidence comfort zone, where thanks to a positive nudge we find we can rise to new challenges and, in doing so, gain more confidence. It takes confidence to move outside your comfort zone, but in doing so you will boost your confidence by demonstrating to yourself that you can handle the unknown.

Natural Confidence

When you start to pay attention to the importance of confidence – both your own self-confidence and that of other people – you'll notice there are different types of confidence and different challenges that people face. Watch how a young child who has been made to feel secure in their world walks into a room and you will see a healthy natural confidence at play.

In adults, natural confidence can show up as a kind of quiet self-possession that, in itself, inspires confidence in others. This is a quality I will be helping you to develop in yourself as you work your way through this book. I will be showing you some simple but powerful NLP Confidence Coaching techniques that you can incorporate into your everyday life to achieve this outcome, encouraging you to pay attention to and record your progress as you make this exciting journey to a more naturally confident you.

To do this we'll need to distinguish between different kinds of confidence. A very good way to start doing this is to use a set of NLP distinctions known as Logical Levels. Logical Levels help us to identify underlying structures and often hidden patterns in our thinking. In short, they help us better understand what is really going on.

Logical Levels of Confidence

There are five basic Logical Levels: Identity, Belief, Capability, Behaviour and Environment. As we work through these, ask yourself at which level you think you'd benefit from having more confidence.

Level 1: confidence at the Identity level

This is confidence in yourself – in who you are – and is what gives you your sense of 'self'. My experience is that as you get to know yourself better, you become more confident in yourself. Indeed, I'd go so far as to say if you truly want to be more confident, one of the smartest things you can do is to develop this relationship with yourself and get to know yourself.

As with any relationship, this is an ongoing process. It takes time and attention, so my question to you is: do you care enough to cultivate this relationship with yourself and take the time and attention it will require?

Many people are scared that if they begin to dig a little deeper, they will find out that what's inside them is not all that pretty – or even downright ugly. I have coached literally thousands of people and I can say categorically that I have yet to come across someone for whom this was true. In fact, it's more usually the case that they are pleasantly surprised by what they find inside. Sometimes they are moved, sometimes they are baffled – but I have yet to work with someone who was terrified or appalled.

This is incredibly important for confidence, because it means you don't have to be on the run from yourself.

A lack of confidence at an Identity level can show up in various ways. I once had a client who was a very successful business-woman and a great cook. She and her husband had chosen not to have children and had been happily married for years when she joined one of our confidence classes. There she let slip that she refused to let her husband cook because if he learnt how to cook, he wouldn't need her any more.

Making sure that others cannot do what you can do is one way of ensuring you are needed, but it's a tough way to live because you're always going to be fearful that you might be rendered surplus to requirements! While my client had loads of confidence in her cooking abilities, she lacked the same confidence in herself.

One of the single most effective ways to become more confident at an identity level is to kick-start a more honest and meaningful relationship with yourself.

Level 2: confidence in your Beliefs

The first question to ask yourself when you start to pay attention to this Logical Level is: do you have beliefs that support you and enable you to function confidently?

If someone says, '*I am a slow learner and will probably never sustain a loving relationship*', they are revealing two distinct beliefs that are unlikely to help them function more confidently in any aspect of their lives.

Someone who believes that '*I am the kind of person who can learn from both my mistakes and my successes*' is telling us they have a belief which will engender confidence. Yes, they will make mistakes; we all do. But they have confidence that they can learn as much from these mistakes as from their achievements. People like this believe in themselves – literally.

However, just saying the words is not enough. Affirmations are not the same as beliefs. Simply saying something does not make it true. If you want to know what a person really believes, pay attention to their behaviour. What they say is one thing; what they do may be quite another.

A belief about the way the world is can support you in your actions. '*I know I have the ability to love again*' is a belief that is more likely to ensure you will recover from a broken relationship and find love again.

Beliefs can be formed at almost any stage of our lives. They are usually a result of our own experiences, which we have tried to make sense of and have drawn conclusions about. But we can also take on the beliefs of significant others in our lives: our parents, our partners and indeed the culture we live in.

In NLP, we talk about belief systems, because you can have all sorts of beliefs. Some may reinforce each other, others may not sit so easily together, especially if formed at different times of your life. Some of your beliefs may even contradict each other, so that when one belief is running you get to be a seven-year-old, when another is running you are thirty-seven, and then you alternate between them. This can be very confusing for anyone who is in any kind of relationship with you!

People will act as if their beliefs are true, but a belief is not a fact. It is simply something that allows us to make sense of our experience. The very function of a belief is to give us some sort of coherent structure to make sense of the world.

As well as helping us make sense of our experiences, beliefs can actually shape what happens to us next because they can become self-fulfilling prophecies. Strangely, whenever this occurs, we tend to take a grim satisfaction in being able to say '*I knew this would happen*' or '*I told you so*'. The satisfaction comes from the fact that our belief about the way the world works has just been proved 'true'. Thus our model of the world makes sense and has just been confirmed in its veracity. We are right – even if we are unhappy. Sometimes people find it hard to let go of being right and embrace the new possibilities that come with new beliefs. As one client said to me recently, 'This really comes down to: do I want to be "right" or do I want to be happy, doesn't it?'

I once worked with a client who had two very bad relationship experiences quite early on in her life and believed, as a result of this, that all men are bad news. This was a belief, not a fact. I know this because unless she had met and checked out every man alive, she could not know for a fact that all men are bad news. But thanks to her beliefs about men, my client kept choosing men who treated her badly. It was only when we challenged and changed this core belief that she could allow herself to find a decent man and a loving relationship.

Level 3: confidence in your Capabilities

When you know that you know *how* to do something, you will automatically approach it with more confidence. If you enjoy cooking, for example, and know you have the basic know-how, you are more likely to be experimental, curious and innovative when you step into the kitchen than someone who hasn't a clue about how to make any kind of meal, never mind a memorable one.

What is it that you already know how to do?

I once put this question to a room full of people and one man, having struggled to think of anything, answered somewhat apologetically that he knew how to go to sleep. Everyone laughed, but I then pointed out that there would be other people in the room and even more outside – in fact, all those who suffered from insomnia – who would love to find out how he was able to go to sleep so consistently.

Ask yourself what you already know how to do but don't, as yet, code as being important and of value. What you find 'easy peasy' is actually a skill set that others may struggle to acquire. They might even pay good money if you could teach them what comes naturally to you.

Knowing *how to* do something can make all the difference between success and failure. NLP has been able to generate an extraordinary number of techniques that enable people to make a change in the way they think and feel. These range all the way from the NLP Spelling Strategy, which can enable just about anyone to spell correctly, to techniques that go to the very heart of our experience as human beings: would it be useful, for instance, to know how to deal with loss, be it of a loved one, a dream, a way of life, a job or whatever? Then the process known as Grief into Gratitude will be extraordinarily helpful. This technique, like all the others, has come about by carefully ascertaining how people who do something successfully do it. What are the steps and what is the best sequence of those steps? This is known as a strategy and it's what gives them the capability. Once we have found this out we can make it available to others. Invariably we can format this as a technique.

Once you start paying attention not just to what you do but how you do it, you may be surprised at how many strategies you already have in place. Often people can then apply these in other settings that previously had not occurred to them. If, for instance, you know how to decide quickly what to have for lunch, that tells you that you have an effective decision-making strategy. It is highly likely that you could apply this same strategy in other areas of your life. If, on the other hand, it takes you forever to decide what to have for lunch, you will want to learn an effective decision-making strategy which you will be able to use not just at lunchtime, but whenever you need to make a decision.

Ask yourself what you would like to know how to do? Begin to ask yourself, specifically, which 'how to's would help you build more confidence? Once you have identified these, start looking for role models whose behaviour demonstrates that they already know how to do what you want to learn. These may be family members, work colleagues, friends or public figures you admire.

Next, you need to hang out with some of these people. So go

and find these people and begin to unpack what it is that they do that makes them consistently successful. One way is to ask them. Another is to role play being them, because it gives you a feel for what it's like to be this way. 'Let's pretend' is how children learn. As they are the most effective learners of all, it would be a smart move to take a leaf out of their book and do what they do – even if you want to call it something a little more grown-up. We could, for instance, call it role play or mental rehearsal. That's what you're doing when you're imagining or trying something on. What would it be like if you could do this? What would it look like? Feel like? Sound like? Cultivate ways of stepping inside someone else's shoes to get the answers to your 'how to' questions.

Level 4: confidence in your Behaviour

What do you want to *do* more confidently? That's what we're talking about when we consider confidence at the level of behaviour.

Behaving brashly or boastfully is not confident behaviour. In fact, it usually signals a want of security and a lack of confidence. Such a lack of confidence can also show up in people not wanting others to learn how to do what they can do.

So what would it be like to behave more confidently? When I ask people this, they invariably talk about feeling self-assured or say they'd be acting like they know what they're doing. In some way, then, the way they behave is a reflection on how they feel about themselves. In terms of Logical Levels their behaviour is connected to their identity. Think about the possibilities this opens up. Change the way you behave and you could end up feeling more confident about yourself at an identity level; change the way you feel about yourself and you could change the way you behave.

To make a change, though, you'll need to get more specific. So what does confident behaviour look, sound and feel like to you? Remember it's got to be your version of confident, one that sits easily with how you behave. Aping someone else's behaviour won't necessarily make you feel more confident; it may just make you feel weird! Of course, the trick is to take what works and make it your own. Do it *your* way.

EXERCISE: Existing Confidence

It's going to be helpful if you can draw on what you already do confidently. So you need to be asking yourself: what do you already do with confidence? I often have clients make a list of at least ten things they do with confidence. What would your ten things be?

1. . . . .
2. . . . .
3. . . . .
4. . . . .
5. . . . .
6. . . . .
7. . . . .
8. . . . .
9. . . . .
10. . . . .

People usually forget the really simple things like . . . walking. You think that's trivial? Just talk to some old people who no longer feel steady on their feet. This is the paradox of confidence. When you've got it, you frequently don't even notice it because you take having an ability for granted. Only when it's in question do you realise how it affects your confidence.

Human behaviour is always a means to an end. One of the best ways to build your confidence is to know why you're doing something – that is, to say what objective you're really aiming for when you engage in a particular behaviour. Frequently this is a powerful motivator. You can see just how powerful when people find themselves in extreme situations. What previously seemed daunting or intimidating now is just what has to be done. Determination, too, can be a great boost to confidence.

One of the ways you can step into this mindset is to read accounts of people placed in situations that required responses above and beyond the norm. Biographies can be extraordinarily revealing. Explorers, for instance, often find they have to do things to survive that go way beyond their everyday experience. The Antarctic explorer Sir Ernest Shackleton is a case in point. Although technically a failure, his 1914 Polar expedition is still studied today as a model of leadership and survival skills, and in particular how a leader can inspire confidence and maintain morale when all seems lost. His ship – aptly named the *Endurance* – was crushed and sunk by the ice. He and his twenty-seven men then endured nineteen months in Antarctica. The crew camped on the frozen surface of the sea for five months. When supplies ran short, Shackleton, with a few other crew members, then made an 800-mile open ocean voyage in lifeboats to South Georgia, trekked over three glaciers and returned to rescue his men. Not a single man was lost.

This was not how Shackleton had imagined the expedition unfolding and it took him to the limit. He most certainly was not confident throughout that all would be well. However, in these changed circumstances, he was very clear about his priority and he made it clear to his men too. He was absolutely committed to bringing them home safely. With this in mind, he was willing to do whatever it took. As he said, 'Difficulties are just things to overcome.'

Shackleton had no choice but to do or die. I'm hoping you have more options! Asking yourself what you're really trying to achieve by engaging in a particular behaviour will sometimes also show you that there are other behaviours that could achieve the same outcome. In this way, you can build a repertoire of behaviours and choose those you feel most confident in doing. Many people will suddenly find the confidence to do something they'd been scared of doing before because they have no choice; they have to. And this holds true for individuals, teams and organisations.

Sometimes people will tell me they want to act more confidently, but when I ask them to be specific they're not sure what that would look like. This is when it can be really useful to imagine the opposite, the worst possible version – i.e. everything you don't want to have happen. Having witnessed a best man speech wrecked by alcohol at a recent wedding he'd attended, Bill was getting nervous about giving his own best man speech at his friend's wedding. So I said to him, 'Suppose you're at a wedding where the best man stands up and wobbles around because he's already drunk too much alcohol. What would be the worst that could happen?' Bill said, 'He can't stop babbling, tells inappropriate stories and jokes, then stops mid-sentence and falls face-first into his half-eaten dinner.'

In the nightmare the best man was already half-cut when he got to his feet, which tells us he was not in the best condition to be addressing a large group of people. In this or any similar situation, you need to think about what is the best state for you to be in and how you can get into that state before you embark on the speech or activity ahead. Because the best man did not manage his state; he couldn't be 'at his best'. If you're smart, you'll ask yourself: when are you at your very best? And how could you reactivate that same state when you may not be feeling as confident?

The nightmare version of the best man fiasco told me what Bill wanted to avoid at all costs. From other things he'd said it was clear that he'd seen many people use alcohol as a crutch. First of all, then, he needed to have enough confidence not to resort to Dutch courage. I asked him what would give him that confidence? He said he needed to know he was ready. I told him that happens most easily when you feel prepared. So it was important he prepared in outline what he was going to say. This also helped him keep to the point. Only after he'd done this did he then come up with a few appropriate anecdotes and jokes. By the time he'd done this, he knew what he was going to say and how he was going to say it.

And there was another very important factor too. Bill needed to get clear about how he was going to finish. Knowing when you're done is every bit as important as knowing how to get started. By the time we were finished he knew how he'd know he was done, and again this added to his overall confidence.

Level 5: confidence in your Environment

The environment you are in will have a huge impact on your confidence and your ability to boost your confidence levels. And by environment, I mean both a physical location and/or a social context.

The important thing to remember is that nobody is confident all the time, and the same applies to the Logical Level of confidence in your environment: nobody is confident in all environments all of the time and you won't be either.

Try this Environment Confidence exercise.

EXERCISE: Confidence in Different Environments

Fill in the lists below to work out where your confidence lies.

Environments I am confident in:

1. ....

2. ....

3. ....

4. ....

5. ....

Environments I am not confident in:

1. . . . .

2. . . . .

3. . . . .

4. . . . .

5. . . . .

Deciding where you want to expend your energy is part of being in control of your life. When you look at contexts you're not confident in, ask yourself: are they all equally important to you? Focus only on those environments that really matter to you. Don't expect to be equally confident, everywhere, all the time. Much like you might increase your repertoire of songs/recipes/contacts, just keep adding to the list at a rate that is comfortable for you.

One of my clients told me how this simple principle had been very useful on her recent holiday in Paris. She had felt scared at the bottom of the Eiffel Tower when thinking about ascending. So confident was the last thing she felt. Then she decided it just wasn't that important to be confident in this environment; it didn't matter, she didn't have to go up. She decided she could still enjoy the experience of seeing one of the world's most famous landmarks close up. Instead, she visited it at night when it's lit up and in some ways is even more magical.

Coming from someone who always pushes herself, this was a very significant decision. When we met after her holiday, she said she wanted to deal with her fear of heights because now she felt ready. Not forcing herself to go up the Eiffel Tower there and then had given her a new confidence to do things at her own pace and in her own time. She's now been up to the top of the tower, but, as she said, 'it was on my terms and not because I felt I had to in order to keep my self-respect'.

From your list, pick one of the environments that you don't

feel confident in and ensure it is one which matters to you. Ask yourself: if I could be more confident in this place, what would I get out of it? Why is this worth bothering with? Here's where you build your motivation. (If you can't come up with anything very compelling here, you might want to ask yourself how important is this really?) Now consider what would need to happen for you to feel more confident in that environment?

When I first met Brian, a recently appointed senior executive, the environment he wanted to feel more confident in was large meetings, to which he would now need to make presentations as part of his new job. He'd not had to do this before and was experiencing real performance anxiety at the prospect. This then was a social environment in the sense that it wasn't a place but the number of people in that place that intimidated him.

Fear of public speaking is probably the most common fear our Confidence Coaches deal with. I run entire programmes on public speaking, so there's a lot that could be said on the subject. But right now I just want to highlight a couple of things I shared with Brian that enabled him to regain his composure.

When people feel intimidated or paralysed in front of groups, they are invariably doing two things. First, they tend to turn their attention inwards, so they're acutely aware of changes in body sensation (such as rapid heart rate) and their internal dialogue. Second, they don't really *see* the people in the audience. This is because they either don't look at them much at all or else they see them as one amorphous mass.

If you don't want to feel scared, you need to stop directing your attention inwards and start directing your attention outwards. You need to pay these people the courtesy of giving them your attention. You can't really do this if you're busy inside your own head talking to yourself or worrying about how you feel physically. Instead, you might want to ask yourself how are *they* feeling and how could you put them at their ease? In the same way, as long as you see them as one big group you intimidate and overwhelm yourself – but you also fail to acknowledge them as people. You need to give these people back their individuality: you need to see the different expressions on their faces and make contact with them as individuals even as they're sitting in this group. That's how you give them their humanity, and when you do that they'll respond to you quite differently. This establishes a relationship between you and them – and this will build your confidence.

Getting to Grips with Logical Levels

Logical Levels give us a set of distinctions to help us identify what's going on for ourselves and others when we face some kind of confidence challenge. Often, the very way people talk tells me what action is needed. The same words said with different emphasis tell me quite different interventions are required. Learning to listen not just to what people say but how they say it will give you a lot of this information, too.

Here's a simple statement: *I can't do that here.* It will have quite different meanings depending on which of these five words the speaker emphasises.

I can't do that here.

Meaning: someone else might be able to do that here, but '*I*' don't have the confidence to. This is the Logical Level of Identity.

*I **can't** do that here.*

Meaning: I don't *believe* that I can do that. This is the Logical Level of Belief.

*I can't **do** that here.*

Meaning: I don't know *how to* do that. This is the Logical Level of Capability.

*I can't do **that** here.*

Meaning: I can't do *that behaviour* here – though I might well be able to do some other behaviour here. This is the Logical Level of Behaviour.

*I can't do that **here**.*

Meaning: I can't do that in *this environment* – but that doesn't mean I couldn't do it in a different environment. This is the Logical Level of Environment.

So, to recap and see for yourself how Logical Levels work in action, think of a challenge you may be facing right now, something that is testing your confidence, and decide which emphasis applies to you.

If you're thinking about an area where you want to be more confident ask yourself: what do I need to change so that I can say, 'I *can* do that here?' At what Logical Level do you need to make a change? Identity? Belief? Capability? Behaviour or Environment? In other words, find out what is holding you back and change it.

Sometimes what's needed is to put your foot on the accelerator; other times we just need to take our foot off the brake.

Confidence in the Universe

We've now explored what's involved in being confident at the level of Environment, Behaviour, Capability, Belief and Identity. Later I want to go beyond Identity and touch on a whole other dimension of confidence.

For now, though, let me give you three questions to ponder:

- Have you ever had a sense of being part of something bigger than yourself?
- Do you find that life has meaning, or that you can give life meaning?
- What would it be like for you to feel confident not just in yourself but in the world that you're a part of?

Outstanding leaders have a confidence that goes beyond confidence in themselves. Invariably they see themselves as being in service of something bigger than them. This can give them a quite extraordinary confidence to go beyond what others believed to be attainable. Connecting to a bigger vision will give you a quite different kind of confidence.

I'll be looking at this bigger picture – and it doesn't get much bigger than the Universe – in Part III: Living with Confidence.

Chapter 3

How to Test Your Confidence

Some people are good at seeing the big picture but not so good at being in touch with what's happening inside them right now. This means they're out of touch with themselves. Other people are only too aware of what's going on inside them – but to the exclusion of almost everything else. Lost in the sensation of the moment, it's hard for them to get any kind of overall perspective. Ideally, we want to be able to do both. And this is a capability – that is, a learnable skill.

To help you cultivate this capability I want to give you two quite different tools which lots of my clients have found incredibly helpful. The Confidence Balance Wheel will help you take stock and see the big picture, while the Confidence Log will give you invaluable feedback about what's going on inside you.

Once we've tried out these tools, I want to alert you to two other critical variables when you're testing your confidence: where praise fits in and how the company you keep can make all the difference.

The Confidence Balance Wheel

We've already seen how confidence is a fluctuating state: how you may be more confident in one area of your life and less confident in another, and that your confidence can and will fluctuate from one day to the next, from one environment to another.

So it's going to be useful to take stock of where and when you have confidence and where and when you need more of it. That's where the Confidence Balance Wheel comes in. This will show you exactly where, right at this moment, you are confident and where you are not.

The areas it focuses on are some of those most commonly raised by clients. It's certainly not a definitive list; there'll be other areas we'll want to focus on later.

Just cast your eye over the wheel for a moment. Then I want to unpack these categories.

The Confidence Balance Wheel illustrating areas of confidence in yourself

Confidence in yourself

There are a couple of things to bear in mind when considering your confidence in yourself. It's not about thinking you're fantastic or that you never screw up. Self-confidence is about being able to be human and know that you've got what it takes, though sometimes you may not feel this way.

If I think about people I've worked with where self-confidence has been a really big issue, there are those who were quite clear that it was their number one problem, but then there were those who had worked hard to conceal this fact – not just from others but often from themselves.

When the latter happens, there are two patterns I've seen arising over and over which are used as attempts to mask the issue. The first of these involves blaming your predicament, whatever it is, on external agents – a tough upbringing, difficult economic circumstances, an abusive boss or partner, and so on. These elements may well be true, but, as I have said to clients over the years, others have faced worse and come through. So what would it take for you to do the same? Having confidence in yourself is almost certainly going to be part of the answer.

The second pattern is to deliberately undershoot – always aiming low so you never fail would be one of the most common ways. Not being ambitious, not daring to dream but instead playing it safe can all be ways of ensuring you don't risk disappointment and potential blows to your self-confidence. Underlying this kind of avoidance strategy is a fear: self-confidence is fragile; it must not be further undermined by setbacks as these will create a feeling of failure – and that could further erode self-esteem.

Confidence in your future

So how do you feel about your future? This is a really open-ended question. People interpret it in different ways: some take a global view, while others focus on particular aspects of their future – e.g. career, relationship. You decide.

You don't need certainty to feel confident. Indeed, sometimes certainty can produce quite the opposite feeling. Imagine three different people: one's just been told they'll be made redundant next month; another that they have a terminal illness; and the third that their partner wants a divorce. Plenty of certainty there, then, and it's going to have a direct impact on the future, but it doesn't necessarily make them feel more confident.

You may not know what lies ahead, but you can still feel confident about the future. So, on a scale of 1 to 10, how confident do you feel?

Confidence in your health

'Right now I don't feel very well, but I know I can trust my body. I'll be fine in a few days.' This is what a client said when he called to say he wanted to do his coaching session by phone rather than in person. He wasn't up to travelling, but if he could stay wrapped up he'd like to go ahead with the session.

Here's someone who takes it for granted that even when he's ill, he has fundamentally good health and will continue to do so. Not surprisingly, this wedge on his wheel scored 8 out of 10. When I asked him why not 10 out of 10, he said there was always room for improvement and that there were some things around diet and exercise he could do that would strengthen his constitution. Right now, though, it wasn't a high priority.

Confidence in your finances

Again, people interpret this is different ways. It's what it means to you that matters.

For some it's about their earning power; for others whether what they're earning is matching their expenditure; for others how things look financially going forward five, ten or twenty years from now, right through to what they will live on when they retire.

But there's another dimension also to consider, which is: how do you feel about financial matters to do with you and those you care for? One client said she'd never been any good at maths at school and that anything to do with finance triggered old school memories of feeling helpless and out of her depth. This was an intelligent woman with a career. Finding she *could* understand some basic principles of personal finance was enormously empowering for her.

So you might want to consider, do you feel like you understand financial matters sufficiently to be able to make informed decisions? Do you feel like you understand what's going on in your financial world? Do you feel like you know what you're doing?

Your social confidence

Whether you're going to a party, going to a public meeting, or just going shopping, these are all social situations and they'll involve a certain degree of social confidence. So how are you with social situations?

Some clients assume that because they tend to be introverts, they can't be socially confident. This just isn't true. You don't need to be a raging extrovert to be socially confident – and here's why.

Social confidence is not about being the life and soul of the party. Nor is it about being all things to all men in some misguided attempt to win the approval of all and sundry. It's about being able to be yourself while at the same time being curious and empathetically interested in others. Empathy is what happens when you step into someone else's shoes. It's the response that's being asked for when people say things like, 'How do you think it is for me?' (By the way, empathy is a learnable skill.) Self-disclosure is the other vital ingredient of social confidence. Only when you're willing to share something of yourself can others get a sense of you. That's enables them to empathise with *you*.

So, on a scale of 1 to 10, how socially confident would you say you are right now?

Your professional confidence

This is not just about whether you feel confident in yourself professionally, but also whether you are able to project and communicate this confidence.

There's an old saying that working actors get work. It points to a profound truth that it's much easier to get what you're going for when you project an air of confidence as it makes others confident in your ability to deliver. This is particularly important in a work setting as it's part of how you convey professionalism and inspire confidence in colleagues, subordinates and those you report to. When you have confidence, you also have a voice and don't just agree out of fear you might otherwise be seen as rocking the boat. So, professional confidence is also about having the courage of your convictions and being real.

One of the best ways to build your professional confidence is to know your strengths and play to them, while at the same time gradually addressing your weak spots. So how professionally confident are you right now?

* * * * *

The Confidence Balance Wheel is an opportunity to let go of being unduly concerned about how things look and assess what is the real state of play at this moment in your life. This is your assessment, not anyone else's, of your confidence level in these different areas. Do acquaintances or family consider you confident? Right now that's irrelevant. This is a means for *you* to decide how confident you feel.

EXERCISE: **Your Confidence Balance Wheel**

Return to the blank wheel on page 44. Rank your level of confidence in each of the confidence segments by giving each a numerical ranking, where zero is very low and 10 is very high. Next draw a straight line in each segment that visually represents that number, if the centre of the wheel is zero and the outer edge is 10.

Here's what one client's wheel looked like:

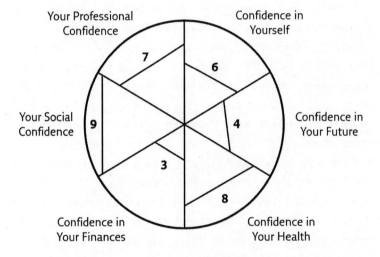

When you've finished this exercise, you will have a blueprint for how your confidence looks and feels right now. If you have a wonky wheel, don't panic. You're normal. This is just a snapshot. Your confidence – and hence the wheel – changes day by day and year by year. Nevertheless it's worth asking yourself if this were a real wheel how bumpy would the ride be?

Most people never get to see all the segments of life at the same time in the way that you have with this Confidence Balance Wheel. That means they don't get to see the big picture and how one aspect of confidence may connect with another in a quite different area of their life. Now that you have a visual representation of the current state of play, let me ask you what strikes you when you look at it? Are you drawn to particular wedges as being particularly important right now?

Very often people begin making connections between what's going on in one domain and another. The example of the client wheel on page 49 is a case in point. This is a real example: Jimmy had been experiencing some acute problems in his business which had hit his finances hard. So his confidence in his finances had really taken a hit – hence the score of 3. Because of the very difficult business climate, he was even more uncertain about the future and had scored that as a 4. These concerns had been with him night and day for almost a year. However, what became obvious to him, looking at his wheel, was that he'd unwittingly narrowed his focus and lost sight of what else he had going for him – strengths that might actually help him deal with the current crisis.

When you're troubled, it's easy to obsess – and this tends to undermine your confidence. Now what struck him was that his health had not suffered at all (8). This kind of surprised him and made him feel stronger in himself even before we did anything concrete about restoring his confidence levels. Socially he was very confident and up for going out and meeting the world (9). He also knew he was really good at what he did and his professional confidence remained high (7).

I then asked him, 'Where would you want to intervene so that if you raised your confidence in that area you'd experience the greatest overall benefit?' He paused, looked at the wheel again and then said, 'I need to know I've got what it takes.'

He'd actually scored his confidence in himself as a 6, which is

twice as high as the 3 for confidence in his finances and a third
more than the 4 he assigned to confidence in the future. There's
an important principle here and it relates to leverage. First, don't
assume that you'll get the most by raising the lowest score.
Second, you may get the biggest return by an apparently indirect
route. As Jimmy said, 'If I'm confident in me and I know I've got
what it takes to bounce back, I'll be fine, then the money will
sort itself out and I'll make a future for myself worth having. I
just need to raise my score to 7 or better still 8.'

Just clarifying things had changed the way he felt about himself and the future. Before he had felt uncertain about what to
do; now it was clear and he had a renewed sense of purpose. This
in itself made him feel more confident. Just raising his confidence in himself score by a single point from 6 to 7 would give
him renewed momentum, and if we could get to 8 he'd feel very
different. He'd also made it clear where, as his Confidence Coach,
I could be of most use to him.

In the rest of this book we'll be looking at how you can boost
your confidence in all of these areas and more.

Keeping a Confidence Log

One of the best ways to kick-start this process is to start a
Confidence Log, which will be your own personal record (and
proof!) of how your confidence and that of those around you
fluctuates and affects how you behave.

Buy yourself a small notebook and carry it with you at all
times for the next ten days so you can make a note of how confident (or not) you feel in all the different situations that crop up
in a normal day. Tracking your reactions can tell you a lot when
you have sufficient data points to see what's going on. So I usually suggest to people that you check in three times in the
morning, three in the afternoon and three in the evening. That

means you'll have nine data points by the end of the day. If you're awake at night, also make a note of how your confidence is then – especially in the wee small hours.

What you are doing is training your brain both to pay attention to and then track a particular class of phenomena that you may not have been very aware of before. In this way you'll start to notice where and when you feel confident, where and when you don't – and where and when your levels of confidence change. In the process you'll become more aware of what helps you to feel stronger and what really boosts your confidence.

Often it is the little things that make the biggest difference, so don't ignore them. In fact, learning to pay attention to the little things is a very important part of training your brain. Think how little it takes to bring you down – a shop assistant is curt or dismissive, say. Too many little things like that can colour your whole day. The reverse is also true: you're friendly to an assistant and they respond with a smile and go out of their way to meet your needs. Suddenly you feel connected and appreciated – and this makes you more confident as you step out into your day.

The best way for me to show you just how useful the Confidence Log can be is to tell you about Jon. Jon came to me for help with building his confidence at work, where he had been struggling for over a year with a very undermining boss.

I asked Jon to make a commitment to keeping his Confidence Log with him throughout the day for ten days and to make a note of his confidence level, depending on the task or interaction he was either facing or engaged in. From the start of his working day – a long, tiring and often difficult commute by car from the countryside to his offices in London – to his return home and his interactions with his wife and family, Jon agreed to keep a log by simply asking himself one question: how confident do I feel right now? He would then give his confidence level a numerical value from zero to 10.

If you do this for yourself and track your confidence over ten days, you'll learn a lot.

Jon added his own refinement which I thought was rather good, so I want to share it with you. Later he would plot his numbers on a graph so that he had a graph for each of the ten days.

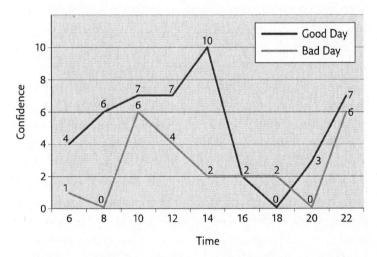

The 'Good Day' graph shows Jon's confidence levels on what he described as a normal working day with no obvious major challenges. But look at the massive fluctuations – and this is on a good day! The 'Bad Day' graph denotes his confidence levels on the day of his first formal appraisal by his boss.

You can see from the graph above that on the difficult day when he knew he would be challenged the scores are much lower. However, even on the day when Jon was not expecting his confidence levels to fluctuate wildly, when he started to pay attention and ask himself *how confident do I feel right now?* he logged significant fluctuations.

Jon told me: 'I was sceptical when I first started because I've always assumed confidence is something you either have or you don't. Something you are born with – or not. I knew I was confident with old friends and less so with new people. I knew I was not as confident as I would like to be at work because it's a new post, and the team I work with are older and more experienced in the field than me.

'What really surprised me was how little things could make such a big difference to how confident I was feeling and how much my confidence went up and down, even in a normal day when I didn't think feeling confident or not would make any difference to me.'

In explaining 'the little things' that had such a big impact on his confidence levels, Jon described how at lunch on the Good Day he'd found himself sitting next to another newcomer to the company, who told him how much he'd enjoyed his presentation of the new project to an audience of 100-plus employees the week before and – guess what? – Jon's confidence level soared to a rating of 10. On the other hand, on the same 'Good Day' he had just completed an important part of the team's joint task, only to sit and watch in horror as his computer crashed and the material he had been working on for a month disappeared. He panicked, tried to retrieve the work and finally called the IT department who had left for the evening. At this point, he rated his confidence in getting the work back and in himself as zero.

However, he called a tech-savvy senior colleague who, somewhat zen-ly, said: 'I'm sure we can get it back in the morning, don't lose sleep over it – what's a month in the entire life of a man?' At this point, Jon rated his confidence in getting the work back as 3 and, more importantly, in himself as 7.

When he woke on the morning of the dreaded performance appraisal, Jon rated his confidence level as 1 and watched it drop to zero as he hit such bad rush-hour traffic that he was late for work. However, once at work he got back in the groove and found himself feeling a bit more himself again, especially when he remembered what his fellow newcomer had said about his presentation at lunch the day before (6). Then came the appraisal (4) and his giving himself a hard time about it afterwards (2) and dwelling on it for some time (2). This was followed by the news that it might not be possible to retrieve the previous month's work after all and this wouldn't become clear for another day (2). On the way home the car broke down and he didn't know how to fix it (0). Talking with his wife, however, he was able to step back from some of this and recognise that he did have something to offer. So he ended the day feeling better about himself (6).

These wild fluctuations really made Jon aware of how volatile his confidence was. This clarified for him where he wanted to go next. He wanted to feel more certain of himself because then he'd be able to weather the storms. So building confidence in *himself* became the focus of our work. And this was extraordinarily fitting because ultimately the only person who could build confidence in Jon was – Jon. Up until then he'd been almost exclusively dependent on the approval of others for his self-esteem. This meant he was very vulnerable to the fear or the threat of it being withdrawn. As he said in a later coaching session, 'I'd been looking for praise, but I'm not sure praise really builds confidence.'

Jon had arrived at an important conclusion, which recent research backs up.

Praise and Confidence

Lots of people – particularly parents – assume they can boost someone's confidence by lavishing them with praise. But American researchers have now shown that, ironically, the wrong kind of praise can be a real confidence-killer.

For the past decade, American psychologist Carol Dweck and her Stanford-based research team have been investigating how kids respond to praise. Her findings will come as an unwelcome surprise to parents who think that simply praising their offspring builds their self-esteem.

In one study, Dweck and her team presented classes of New York fifth-graders with a range of non-verbal intelligence tests and then randomly divided them into two groups; praising one group for their *intelligence* and the other for the *effort* they made when tackling the tests. Each group was then given the same choice between two more tests, one of which was clearly harder than the other. Over 90 per cent of the pupils who had been praised for their *effort* in the previous test opted for the harder one, while the majority of the kids who had been praised for their *intelligence* copped out and took the easier test.

Dweck concluded: 'When we praise children for their intelligence, we tell them that this is the name of the game. Look smart, don't risk making mistakes.' And that's exactly what the fifth-graders had done by choosing the easier second test. They had chosen to look smart and avoid the risk of being embarrassed. Being told you are clever, whether you are five, fifteen or fifty years old, does not automatically instil confidence. By contrast, being told you did a good job trying – that is, being praised for your effort – not only builds confidence but can spur you on to try an even bigger challenge. Being confident does not mean you will no longer make mistakes; it means you will know you can have a go and handle the outcome whether it is positive or not.

In further studies on the impact of praise on children, Dweck also discovered some unpleasant truths about over-praised youngsters, namely that they are more interested in tearing others down. When, for example, students were given two puzzle tests and, after completing the first test, were offered a choice between learning a new puzzle strategy for the second test or finding out how they did compared with their classmates on the first test, students praised for their intelligence wanted to know their class ranking instead of preparing for the second test. Those praised for their effort gamely took the new test.[1]

When school kids move up to a new level of education, many who have done well up to this point struggle in a larger, more demanding environment. Those who have equated their previous success with innate ability can sometimes really suffer and end up believing maybe they were dumb all along. Their grades never recover because the one thing that could get them back on track – making more effort – is seen as further proof of their failure. This is the point when in interviews with the researchers, many of these intelligent students admit they would seriously consider cheating. This is a telling indicator of a lack of confidence – they believe they need some added advantage because they're insufficient on their own.

The ability to respond to disappointment or even failure by making more effort is a well-studied psychological trait. Those who have this persistence rebound well and can maintain their motivation through long periods of delayed gratification. Why? Because they have the confidence that, eventually and through increasing their efforts, they will succeed.

That means they can rely on themselves and they feel up to competing with others. For this reason, a truly confident person has no need to undermine others. Similarly, for them, cheating would actually be undermining because it would prove that they couldn't achieve under their own steam.

The Company You Keep

As we have just seen from Jon's Confidence Log, the company you keep can have an enormous impact on your confidence. Ask yourself: what impact are the people I hang out with having on my confidence levels? Do they keep me where I am? Do they drag me down? Do they take me higher?

When Vivienne first came to me for coaching, she had just walked out of a high-profile job as a contract journalist on a national newspaper, a job others would have killed for.

It was clear the decision to quit had not been an easy one.

Vivienne had been in the post for eight years, had earned a reputation as a specialist at the top of her field, was the sole breadwinner in her family at that time and yet had pulled the plug on not only her financial security but also her sense of 'self'. I was intrigued. I had just one question for Vivienne. Why?

'To the outside, it looked as if I had it all,' she told me. 'It was a great job, and I had worked like a donkey for twenty years to land it but – and it's a big but – it came at a price and I no longer wanted to pay that price.' That price was the serious impact it was having on her confidence.

'The editors that I worked for felt they had "made" me – and made it clear they could just as easily "break" me,' she told me. 'They did not acknowledge the work I had invested to become an expert in the field but operated from a sense of sour grapes. After all, they had to clock in and out of an office and for all they knew, I spent my days having manicures and long lunches, stopping only to bash out my column in my sleep. I knew they were keeping me where I was and actively preventing me from going any further in my career.

'My column was an enormous success and made a lot of money for the companies I wrote about and recommended. I had worked very hard behind the scenes to make my name, but it suddenly felt as if I had become everyone's best friend, not for me but for what I could do for them. I could not even have coffee with people without them pitching at me. In the end, I woke up one morning, unplugged my office telephone, changed my email address and quit my job. I spent the rest of that day crying. I was so sad, but between the sour grapes and the hounding for more and more publicity, I knew I did not want to carry on.'

When I first met Vivienne, she was struggling with the loss of identity that had accompanied her shock resignation: doors that used to swing wide open were now firmly shut and the phone had stopped ringing. But she was adamant she did not regret her decision to quit.

'I still have all the skills I spent twenty years honing, I now know when my phone rings it is likely to be someone who actually cares about me – not what they can get out of me – and although I'm broke and it's not easy to find work, I know I will survive. I'm just better off without those people in my life.'

It was not the high-profile job that gave Vivienne the confidence in herself, it was having the courage to walk away from it. Only then was she able to go towards a different kind of life and spend time with people who valued her and actually created new writing opportunities for her. Thus she is now successfully paying her mortgage.

Self-confidence is an inner strength and a faith in yourself. Frequently, this is born out of the most apparently unlikely circumstances. Sometimes it is when people have been most under pressure and feeling anything but confident that they lay the foundations for such confidence. True confidence frequently comes out of adversity: you rise to the challenge; you survive; you may even thrive. So gruelling circumstances can actually build your confidence – because you find you did have what it takes to come through.

PART II

APPLIED CONFIDENCE

Chapter 4

Developing 4×4 Confidence

The great thing about 4×4 vehicles is that they are all-weather, all-terrain vehicles. Ideally that's what you want your confidence to be like, too. To achieve this kind of rugged performance that you can rely on, we may need to do some Confidence Engineering.

Using the Confidence Balance Wheel we were able to identify some of the most common areas in which confidence issues show up and how things presently stand for you. People often play to their strengths and avoid their weaknesses, but this is unlikely to build all-round confidence; you just get more and more confident about the things you were already confident about.

Four-wheel-drive and all-wheel-drive vehicles have an automotive drive system in which mechanical power is transmitted from the drive shaft to all wheels. That gives you incredible versatility and much greater control, whatever the driving conditions.

If you want to feel like you're in the driving seat, you'll want the same kind of versatility in your confidence as you navigate the road of life. That's why I want to introduce you to what builds – or destroys – confidence. These are the bases you need to hit if you're going to boost your confidence on a permanent basis.

First, I want to introduce you to the Four Pillars of Confidence, which support pretty much everything we do that enhances confidence. Then I will familiarise you with the Four Confidence Keys.

Focus first on the pillars, then on the keys, and you really can create 4×4 confidence.

The Four Pillars of Confidence

If you want to experience true and lasting confidence – and all the benefits that come with it – you need to recognise that your physical, mental, emotional and spiritual confidence are all equally worthy of your attention because any one of these can affect the other three. Here's what they are and here's what you can do.

Pillar 1: physical confidence

In good health, physical confidence is something most of us can and do take for granted. But when illness strikes or if we're involved in an accident, the loss of confidence can be sudden and shattering. The impact is not as great, though, if you already have something in each of your other accounts in the confidence bank.

When I visited my dentist recently, she told me about her elderly mother, who for the last eight years had been confined to her home since 'she had her accident'. Her mother had tripped on the path leading to her front door and broken her wrist. 'She's never been the same since. She lost all her confidence and in many ways, it seems like it gets worse the more time that goes by,' my dentist told me. 'She used to lead such an active life and now we can barely persuade her to leave the house.'

Instead of time, that 'great healer', helping this woman recover from the shock of the accident so that she could return to her former, more confident self, the more time that had passed, the less confident she had become.

What had been a physical shock to begin with had affected her in pretty much every area of her life. In an attempt to protect herself, she had withdrawn into an ever smaller world. Eight years later, the only safe place was her home. There is an important lesson here for us all and it is this: any loss of confidence can get bigger and bigger and have a long-term, life-changing impact, especially if you try to just ignore it.

While it makes sense to choose your time to act and to ensure that you are as prepared as possible, a rule of thumb I tell my clients is that avoidance is the enemy of confidence.

So what might build your physical confidence? For one of my clients it was learning how to do cartwheels and being able to jump over a five-bar gate! Both of these things he'd been unable to do as a kid and had watched in awe as other children had done them. When he learnt as an adult that he too could do these things, he found a new sense of security in his body because he knew he too could master physical skills. As he put it, 'I don't feel a wimp any more.' It was unfinished business from childhood and definitely changed both the way he felt about his body and his physical self-image. It didn't actually take that long to master both skills but it gave him enormous satisfaction – and greatly increased his overall confidence.

What would do this for you? What physical challenges could you rise to that would give you a new way of recognising what your body is capable of when you invest some time and attention in it? For one client it was ballroom dancing; for another juggling. In both cases they got to feel differently in their body but they also got to feel differently about their body. And this made them feel differently about themselves.

One of the best ways to develop, boost and maintain physical confidence, whatever your starting point, is to make a decision to engage with your own body. You can do this in a thousand different ways. You could, for instance, notice which foods make you feel tired and which give you more energy; what time of day you feel at your best; what is physically pleasing to you – massage, walking, running or something else?

Instead of taking for granted that you will stay in a healthy state, invest in your future now. Again this can be done in lots of ways and it doesn't have to be a big deal. Each morning, when I'm getting dressed, I deliberately put my socks on while standing up, simply because it's a great way to improve your balance. When I first started doing this, it was often quite comical to watch. Now it's pretty smooth. I find that encouraging, because balance is critical to physical well-being. (Loss of balance is one of the major causes of injury to old people.)

Exercise and physical self-care will not only support your current physical well-being, they will also boost your confidence that you can enjoy good health.

Pillar 2: mental confidence

Mental confidence is not about making mindless affirmations which you then expect to come true magically. (Paradoxically, affirmations can actually undermine confidence if you keep telling yourself you can do something and keep finding you can't.)

Your mental confidence level is directly affected by your internal dialogue and the movies you run in your mind. So it's going to be useful if you have tools to address both.

I cannot stress enough that our tone of voice, the words we use and the belief system our internal voice is reinforcing will have a profound effect on how confident we feel. If that voice is saying, 'Oh God, I've screwed up again – big time. Why do I always do this? What's wrong with me?' then it is not supporting your desire to build or even maintain your confidence. But there's a lot you can do to change this.

One of my clients was plagued by negative internal dialogue – it even kept him awake at night! When I asked him where the internal voice was located, he looked puzzled for a moment and then pointed to the right side of his head. I suggested he move the voice to the left side of his head. As soon as he did so he smiled; he was surprised at the difference this made. Next I suggested that he experiment with moving the voice one foot out from this point on the left side. He let out a big sigh: 'Now I don't feel overwhelmed.' When he moved the voice two feet out, he found that both the volume and tone changed. The internal dialogue was quieter and more pleasant to listen to: 'it doesn't feel critical any longer'. Now he could listen to what was being said and rationally assess whether or not it was a valid point of view.

Technically these mini-interventions are known as sub-modality adjustments (for more on NLP Sub-Modalities, see page 105). We were making changes to the auditory modality. The location, distance, pitch and volume are all sub-components of any auditory experience and that's what we were tweaking. I've lost count of the number of times these simple interventions have had the most profound impact on people. In the same way, you might want to get curious about your own internal dialogue – not just what you're saying, but how you're saying it.

The person who is really in charge of your mental confidence is not the boss who sacked you, the spouse who left you or the teenager who told you they hated you. The person who can determine just how mentally confident you are and how mentally confident you can stay is you. What you tell yourself – your internal dialogue – and how you depict it in your mind – your mental movie – is going to make all the difference.

We can make similar profound adjustments to your mental movie. Choose something that had, and may still be having, a big impact on you. It could be an argument with a work colleague, the final conversation with an ex-partner or being told you were going to be made redundant from your job.

Now replay this scenario in your mind's eye. See which of the following visual sub-modality changes have the most impact for you:

- Run the movie in colour.
- Run the movie in black and white.
- Run the movie in sepia.
- Imagine turning a dial to make the movie 'brighter' in your mind.
- Imagine turning a dial to make the movie 'darker' in your mind.
- Zoom in on the scenario, bringing it closer to you.
- Reverse this: zoom out and move the scenario further away.
- Make the movie a still photograph.
- Make the movie very clear and sharply defined.
- Make the movie out of focus.

As you make these changes, notice the different effects each one has on you. Different changes affect people differently, so it's useful to find out what is most powerful for you. That said, there are some rules of thumb which hold true more often than not.

By running the scene in sepia, making it darker, moving it further away, imagining it as still or out of focus, you will find a scene usually has less impact and is less upsetting than when you imagine it in full colour, brightly lit, close up and clearly in focus.

By using those sub-modalities that make the scenario appear old and distanced from you, you have learned how to show yourself that this experience is something that has happened. It is in the past. It is not some kind of on-going nightmare. It is not happening now. Which means that when you do think about it in this 'distanced' way, it will have far less impact on you and will not shatter your confidence all over again.

What you're doing here is employing the craft of the cine-matographer. By being your own director, you get to make your own movies – ones that really work for you.

Pillar 3: emotional confidence

Fluctuating internal states or emotions, good and bad, pleasant and unpleasant, are a normal part of being human. Being emo-tionally confident means being confident enough to experience the whole range of emotions without being terrified you might be overwhelmed by one in particular.

If you want to boost your emotional confidence, it's going to be useful to consider which states and emotions you are least comfortable with, because these are probably the ones you do your best to avoid – and that probably means that in your quest to avoid those feelings you probably avoid doing certain things, thus limiting your behavioural choices.

You may have witnessed someone turning white with fear or red with anger. You may have felt yourself stiffen with appre-hension and then relax as you receive the reassurance you need to know you are safe and all is well. Our bodies respond to our emotions and betray them even if we would prefer to keep our feelings hidden. When we are truly confident, we can stop trying to hide our feelings; we can express them in a healthy and pos-itive way.

It is a sign of being emotionally confident that you are not afraid to be afraid, that you know sadness and grief serve a heal-ing purpose and will, with time, pass and that being angry will not turn you into the Incredible Hulk.

To boost your emotional confidence, you simply need to have the courage to allow yourself to experience those emotions and then allow them to pass.

One of the confidence tools I created which people have found particularly useful is what I call your baseline state. This is where you hang out internally most of the time. Sometimes there can be big events which give you big state changes and big feelings, but your baseline state is what feels most familiar: the norm to which you revert when nothing out of the ordinary is going on. Whether it's pleasant or not, it is at least familiar and so becomes part of who you think you are.

Jan came to see me because she felt anxious much of the time. This anxiety was her baseline state. She told me how she had felt this way ever since she was a child and spending a lot of time with her mother. But when she said, 'I'm a very anxious person,' I really didn't think it was useful for her to be taking this state on at an Identity level, so I said, 'Are you sure?' She looked puzzled. It was clear that my question had got her attention. So then I asked her, 'When you're feeling anxious, who does this remind you of?' Without hesitation she immediately said, 'My mother.' I then asked her, 'So whose anxiety is this?' Her answer changed her life: 'My mother's!'

What had been her baseline state for most of her life wasn't even her own! Like every child, she had been a brilliant learner and learned how to do anxiety from an expert. Jan had assumed this baseline state was pretty much hardwired and thus part of who she was. Now we could begin to explore how she might be if she started being herself.

It has never occurred to most people that the way they are used to feeling is something they can modulate – and that the way they have got used to feeling is not necessarily how they need to spend the rest of their life feeling.

So take a moment and consider how do you feel most of the time? That's your current baseline state. Is it working for you? Would you like to enhance it or perhaps completely change it? Either way, knowing what triggers it is going to be really useful – but so is knowing which triggers give you more of the feelings you'd prefer. This is where paying attention to the triggers in your life can be so useful – and then making sure you get more of the good ones.

Let me ask you to consider for a moment:

- What makes you feel most alive?
- What raises your spirits?
- What brings you joy?

Are there enough of these things in your life right now? Add more of these with any consistency and you will change your baseline state for the better. When you enhance your baseline state, you strengthen the foundations of your confidence.

Pillar 4: spiritual confidence

When you have spiritual confidence you know what you're about, because you know what matters to you, why it's important and what your purpose is; this makes life meaningful to you and gives you direction.

I have often found that no matter how successful a person is they frequently don't feel fulfilled until they engage with this area of life. And it's really quite easy to do so. I can best show you by asking you what I ask them and exploring some of the aspects that arise by talking candidly from my own experience.

The payoff from having this spiritual confidence is that you'll have the courage to keep pursuing what really matters to you. You won't necessarily have the answers or always know what to do, but you'll have the confidence to trust which way to go.

So where to begin? I often start by asking a person: 'What do you find inspiring?' For me, it is seeing people really come into their own, and become more of who they really can be. Even after all this time, it's what makes me wake up early with excitement on those days when I know I'm going to be running a programme where this will once again start happening in front of my eyes. Over the last thirty years, I've created many vehicles to do this, some open to the public, some not. To do this I've entered into business arrangements with all sorts of people and organisations. Some have worked incredibly well and continue to do so; others didn't. In the process, I've seen the best and the worst of people.

At times I have felt betrayed, but that has never affected my fundamental belief that if you just give people a safe environment and the tools to engage with themselves they will begin to come home to themselves – and that as they do so they will find that they need to be doing something with their life that matters to them. In short, they will want to live a life of intention and purpose – and that means they'll want to start shaping their life.

For me, this is a spiritual mission – to create the context in which people can rise to their magnificence. Everything I do is driven by this. My team often tell me that it's tough keeping up with the number of initiatives I want to launch. Some of them work; some of them don't. When they don't, I can feel disappointed but I never lose sight of why we're engaged in these activities. They are only ever a means to this end. (The same is true of NLP.) And that gives me a particular kind of confidence to just keep going. This is my spiritual confidence.

Too often people confuse spiritual with religious. I've met some very religious people who didn't seem to me to be at all spiritual. I've also known some people who I felt were deeply spiritual who had no religious affiliation at all. Then there are the people who aren't so much spiritual as evangelical. They get evangelical about whatever has worked for them and think everyone should do it. This can be virtually anything. Over the years, I've seen a few people try to turn NLP into the answer to everything. For me, though, it's very simple: NLP is a very good servant but it would make a poor master. Why? Because, like any technology, and any way of thinking, it needs to be in service of something bigger than itself.

If you think about how the word spirit is used, you can get a sense of this deeper meaning. Here are a few examples:

He honoured the spirit of the agreement, not just the letter of the law.
Everything he did was in the spirit of his teacher's wishes.
That was a very spirited rendition.
His words inspired her to excel.
What she had to say was truly inspiring.

What is it to inspire? According to Merriam-Webster's online dictionary, it is 'to exert an animating, enlivening, or exalting influence'. That's not surprising when you consider that the 'spirit' in the word spiritual and the word inspire have the same etymological root: they come from the Latin for 'to breathe'.

In fact, there are a whole load of words in English where this breathing – this life-giving principle – is at play: respiration is to re-spire or breathe again; to conspire is to breathe together; aspire literally means rough breathing; to transpire is to go across or beyond through the breath; to expire happens when you finally breathe out; and to inspire is to breathe in.

When people are able to feel they are living with purpose, they experience feeling alive in a whole different way. They are able to prioritise easily because some things take them in the direction that is meaningful to them, while other things won't – and consequently can seem less important even trivial.

To do this they need to know what matters to them. So your values become critical. Often people aren't sure what these are when we begin. Nevertheless, they are always there just waiting to be put into words. One way to do this is to notice what makes you angry. What makes you angry violates your values. So, if seeing people being bullied makes you mad, then you clearly have some values about how people should be treated.

Once you know what matters to you, the next step is to start living those values. The more you do this, the more you'll feel at home in your own skin. You'll also feel all of a piece more of the time, rather than internally conflicted. Why? Because you're being true to yourself and what really matters to you. Living your values means you'll also want to find work that isn't at odds with them.

So as I said, what do you find inspiring? Get more of those things in your life and I can guarantee you will experience a new kind of confidence. This spiritual confidence will give you a new lease of life because you'll be breathing new life into yourself.

Your Four Confidence Keys

From its earliest days NLP has focused on looking at what works, wherever it may be found. This makes it both a very inclusive but also a very rigorous approach: inclusive because we're interested in whatever works, wherever it comes from; rigorous because we're only interested if an approach actually works and can deliver worthwhile results.

Gathering information and surveying the field is a smart thing to do if you want to draw on the combined experience and expertise of those who have gone before you and those who are currently working in the field. One NLP filter to apply is: what works best? This filter enables you to distil what is critical, while avoiding getting bogged down in tribal allegiances to any one particular approach.

I want to share with you four keys to confidence that emerge when you do this.

Confidence key 1: optimism

Optimism is faith that leads to achievement. Nothing can be done without hope or confidence ... No pessimist ever discovered the secret of the stars, or sailed to unchartered land, or opened a new doorway for the human spirit.

Helen Keller

The American psychologist Professor Martin Seligman is often called the father of positive psychology – the study of optimal human functioning – which asks the question: what makes happy and well people the way they are and what interventions will support people being happy and well? Seligman suggests that: 'The basis of optimism does not lie in positive phrases or images of victory, but in the way you think about causes'.

He has defined this as 'explanatory optimism', giving us a new way of understanding the roots of optimism: 'Each of us has our own explanatory style; a way of thinking about the causes of things that happen in our lives. We develop our explanatory style in childhood and, unless deliberate steps are taken to change it, it will last for the whole of our life, acting as a prism through which we explain to ourselves why things, good or bad, happen to us.'[2]

Seligman argues that three dimensions are particularly important in determining how we explain events to ourselves, and therefore what meaning we make of them: permanence, pervasiveness and personalisation.

Optimism is a learnable thinking skill. It is worth checking out how these three dimensions currently show up in your life. Why? Because if you become more optimistic, you will undoubtedly become more confident.

Permanence: permanent v. temporary (how long is it going to last?)

A person who has a pessimistic explanatory style will assume that when something goes wrong, this is 'the norm', that it will persist and will always be there to adversely affect their life. This gives rise to a feeling of helplessness. When good things happen, pessimists will explain these events in ways that suggest they are the result of transient causes, even moods, that can't be relied on.

By contrast, someone whose explanatory style is optimistic

will see setbacks as temporary. They'll tell themselves that even if it has gone wrong this time, it will go better next time. This gives them great resilience. And when good things happen, their explanations invariably attribute these results to permanent causes like their own character traits and abilities.

Pervasiveness: specific v. global (how widespread is this?)

Pessimists tend to see unwanted events as having a global explanation ('It's always this way'). So they'll often generalise ('People always ...') and even catastrophise ('It can only get worse and here's what would be even worse'). Optimists don't like failure either, but they will see it as a special case, an exception to the norm. Failure has a specific cause ('That particular business decision was mistaken but I still know how to make good decisions.')

And when things go right? Pessimists see success as very specific and limited to a particular skill set and context ('I'm good at remembering names, that's all'). Optimists see good events as natural and of global import in their lives. They attribute success to a trait that applies universally ('I've always got on with people').

Personalisation: internal v. external (is it me or them?)

This is about who to blame when things do go wrong. Pessimists blame themselves and internalise the problem; optimists will tend to blame others or events outside their control, thus externalising the cause.

People who blame themselves are likely to have low confidence levels, whereas those who can find external explanations for why something has gone wrong generally feel more positive about themselves and have higher levels of confidence.

It doesn't take much imagination to see how these different response patterns will impact upon our confidence and self-esteem. Everyone is going to experience setbacks; how you explain them to yourself will determine the meaning they have for you and how you feel about yourself. This doesn't mean you won't have self-critical thoughts or feel down sometimes. But optimistic causal explanations give you the power to act in your life; instead of feeling helpless you can do something to change things from hereon in.

Pessimism has a high cost associated with it. Often pessimists experience a certain inertia in the face of adversity; they don't have the get-up-and-go of optimists. They also risk suffering increased ill health, both physical – through suppressed immune system functioning – and mental – through greater susceptibility to depression.

Take negative internal dialogue – what we say to ourselves on the inside – which often goes with setbacks. Two different – and learnable – strategies are common: distraction and disputation. Optimists tend to engage with negative internal dialogue quite differently from pessimists. Sometimes they will just think of something else which means they don't go round and round and keep on berating themselves. However, by far the most effective strategy optimists exhibit is that they will actually begin arguing with any self-limiting thinking. That means they challenge their own internal dialogue.

Though some people do this intuitively, its availability as a learnable strategy is really down to the pioneering work of US psychologist Albert Ellis, the father of Rational Emotive Behaviour Therapy. Ellis argued that anxiety and depression were often the result of distorted thinking and that by developing rational, healthier beliefs, we could experience rational and healthier emotions. Say an adverse event occurs. This activates our belief system which triggers a consequent emotion. Different people can respond quite differently to the same experience depending on the beliefs that they bring and foster.[3]

The pessimist's experience:

Activating event: Your boss says your work is
                           unsatisfactory.

Belief: I just don't have what it takes.
                           I'm useless.

Consequent emotion: Self-doubt leading to anxiety
                        culminating in depression.

The optimist's experience:

Activating event: Your boss says your work is
                           unsatisfactory.

Belief: I did my best. It wasn't all bad anyway
                           so I know I could probably do better
                           next time.

Consequent emotion: Disappointment, but confident about
                        being able to improve.

The Ellis ABC model is a great tool for fostering optimism. It has been refined and added to over the years. In some versions we're now up to the letter E. Briefly, the ABC Model states that we all experience things just about every day of our lives that can be **Activating events** (A). These can range from the trivial (you cannot find the car keys) to life-changing (job loss, divorce, death of a loved one). Trivial or major, these events will prompt thoughts that become **Beliefs** (B) about the event, the circumstances surrounding it and our role in it. These trigger **Consequent emotions** (C).

To overcome unhelpful beliefs (I couldn't find the car keys because the whole world is against me!) we need to use **Disputation** (D), which means not accepting this pessimistic explanatory style. As we succeed in challenging unhelpful beliefs, we feel **Energised** (E): more optimistic – and therefore more confident – about our lives.

Like pretty much anything else, optimism can also be

contextual – that is, more apparent or developed in some contexts than others. It's possible that we may be more optimistic in some areas of our life than others. Back to the Confidence Balance Wheel again! Take a look at yours and ask yourself whether you're able to handle setbacks in some areas better than in others. According to Professor Seligman, there are also significant differences between the sexes, which, he suggests, may explain why men tend to rise higher up the career ladder than women. He says men are more optimistic about work, blaming failure on temporary, local and external factors, but they are pessimistic about relationship failures, blaming permanent, pervasive and personal causes. Women are the exact opposite, pessimistic about achievement but optimistic about social setbacks.

Optimism is not some foolish Pollyanna-like determination to believe things will always turn out for the best. It's a causal explanation. We now have two decades of research to demonstrate that the benefits of adopting a more optimistic outlook on life include not only a happier and more confident life, but a longer one!

Research led by psychologist Dr Mika Kivimaki, who is based at the Finnish Institute of Occupational Health, National Research and Development Centre for Welfare and Health, has shown how optimism can also reduce the risk of health problems and actually help a person recover after the shock of a serious, life-changing event such as the death of a spouse or a child or the loss of their job. Following a major life crisis, pessimists take more time off work than optimists and run a very real risk of giving up in the face of adversity by telling themselves – and passively accepting – they were born to draw the short straw in life.

'We don't need to live like this,' says Dr Kivimaki. 'When bad things happen, we should take action by striving to find the "not me", "not always" and "not everything" explanations and then focus our energy there. For some people, this could mean the difference between life and death!'[4]

Interestingly, when you have an optimistic causal explanatory model, you'll also be more able to confront your fears. Research shows that optimists tend to pay more attention than pessimists to information that will help them reduce health risks. A study by Lisa Aspinwall, associate professor at the University of Utah, found that when subjects were given information about cancer and other serious health issues, optimists spent more time than pessimists reading the 'severe risk' material and remembered more of it.

She concluded: 'It is because they are optimistic they are prepared to bite the bullet and spend time attending to major health risks. These are the people who aren't just sitting around wishing things were different. They believe in a better outcome, and that whatever measures they take will help them to heal.'[5]

Whether you are an optimist or a pessimist, you are forming your view of the world and how it works. Seen in terms of Logical Levels, your explanatory style has profound implications. It will shape your Beliefs. These in turn will influence your sense of self (your Identity), which will affect what you believe you have the skills and abilities (your Capabilities) to do (your Behaviour) and where and when (Environment) it's going to be possible. As we saw in Chapter 2, a belief is not the same as a fact – which means it is never too late to change your beliefs and thus learn to be more optimistic.

Studies of twin populations reveal that between 25 and 50 per cent of our key personality traits – including levels of optimism – are inherited from our parents. So the good news is that you can work on the other 50 to 75 per cent to increase your optimism. Good news for pessimists who want to become optimistic, but also for born optimists who want to develop more optimism in specific areas of their life.

EXERCISE: **Optimism Builder**

Pick an event that is currently troubling you.

Part 1

Briefly write down in a single sentence for each:

1. (a) The activating event (i.e. what triggered things for you).
2. (b) What you believe as a result of this event (e.g. what you're telling yourself).
3. (c) Your consequent emotion (i.e. how you feel as a result whenever you think of this).

Part 2

Ask yourself:

4. How long is this issue going to last?
5. How widespread is it?
6. Is this down to me, or others, or a combination of both?
7. Is my internal dialogue and movie-making helping or hindering?

Part 3

8. Make the necessary sub-modality adjustments to your internal dialogue and mental movie as outlined in Mental confidence (see page 81) so that both support you.
9. Through what you tell yourself (your internal dialogue), the movies you run in your mind and the feelings that both engender, begin to create alternative positive futures that make sense to you as possibilities you can work towards.

Confidence key 2: resilience and perseverance

More than education, more than experience, more than training, a person's level of resilience will determine who succeeds and who fails. That's true in the cancer ward, it's true in the Olympics, and it's true in the boardroom.

Dean Becker, *Harvard Business Review*, May 2002

Boosting your confidence does not mean you will never again suffer any form of self-doubt, but it does mean you will be better able to handle disappointment and even failure. How well you can do this will depend in part on your resilience.

No matter how confident you are, you will still find there are tough times. We all need to be able to take the knocks in life – and you can be sure there *will* be knocks: trying to avoid them is akin to running away from life itself.

If someone is resilient, they're not just tough. They'll certainly have stamina, but more than this, they're able to bounce back. To be resilient is to be irrepressible, whatever life throws at you. Some people are more resilient than others. Sometimes you will likely feel more – or less – resilient. Noticing what helps you feel resilient and what undermines this feeling is going to be really useful information.

Let me tell you about the research on this subject. Psychologists Karen Reivich and Andrew Shatté, co-authors of *The Resilience Factor*, suggest there are seven learnable skills which will enable you to be much more resilient:

1. Learning your ABCs. They argue that the primary roadblock to resilience is your thinking style.
2. Avoiding thinking traps, such as blaming others and jumping to conclusions when things go wrong.
3. Detecting iceberg beliefs that float under the surface of your mind and which may be working for you or against you.

4. Learning how to challenge your own beliefs so that you can test their validity and usefulness.

5. Knowing how to put things in perspective, rather than turning every mishap into a potential catastrophe.

6. Having the means to calm and refocus yourself when you're knocked off balance.

7. Being able to achieve resilience in real time as and when needed.

When you look at this list, how many of these would say you know how to do? Each is a learnable skill and Reivich and Shatté's book, which I recommend reading, offers plenty of practical tips for how to improve your own abilities in all seven areas.

The way you start to build resilience and an ability to bounce back is by playing to the strengths you already have. You don't need all seven qualities to become more resilient, you simply need to work out what you already do and then begin adding the others.

Some people have their own techniques that work really well for them. One client told me how when something didn't go well she would make a movie of it afterwards in her mind's eye and see herself in it. As she watched from a safe distance she would wonder what she could learn from this particular movie. Once she knew, she would run it backwards very fast until she no longer felt defeated by the episode. This is a brilliant application of a whole host of NLP principles. Years before, she'd been on a one-day course of mine and had seen me use the NLP Fast Phobia Cure. She'd then modified the technique for her own purposes and found it served her very well.

Another client told me how when the going gets tough, he simply lies down for five minutes. He is literally grounding himself. It doesn't matter to him whether it's on a bed or the floor: 'it helps me regroup and take stock. I come back to myself'. Far from running away, he's getting ready to resume control.

I've worked with a lot of entrepreneurs and many have suffered great reversals of fortune. It's the ones who can bounce back that are able to stay the course and ultimately succeed.

One of them, Benjamin, found that when his first business went into receivership, his wife also left him. One of the reasons she gave was that he was sexually boring and she couldn't stand doing the same thing any longer. This double whammy would have crushed a lot of people. His response was different. He was determined to bounce back from the business failure. Sure enough, within five years he was running a new business and was also a millionaire. What came out of the coaching, though, was that he also began to believe there was no reason why he couldn't apply the curiosity that worked for him in business to help him find out how to become more sexually interesting. Certainly he was hurt – but he was also critical: 'Why didn't she say something?' He started getting curious about what a woman would want from him sexually. When his wife began to admit she was having second thoughts about their parting, it was Benjamin who said the moment had passed. He had a new woman and he was learning just how good sex could be – for both of them!

Given that life will not go as you might always hope or expect, resilience gets to be a critical feature of successful – and confident – living.

So what do you *already do* that builds your resilience? Suppose this was just part of your everyday life, rather than something you did only *in extremis*. Then, as with good nutrition, you're just laying a foundation for success that makes whatever the day brings that much more manageable because you've got a lot in reserve. Maybe you prefer to do something physical. For me, strength training with my trainer is like this – plus, if I'm actually dealing with something tough just before doing it, it never fails to make me feel more resilient there and then. I think it works because it refocuses my attention and requires all of me to pull together to achieve the goal of the next pull-up. Also, even as I burn off any excess stress hormones, I'm put in touch again with my strength and I finish with a completely different hormonal chemistry. And you? Some people just go for a walk and feel entirely different afterwards. Others spend time with friends so they feel connected and supported.

In my experience of working with clients, there are three particularly valuable qualities I associate with resilience:

1. Resilient people have a high tolerance of ambiguity and do not rush to make decisions. They have impulse control. This makes them much more masters of their own destiny.
2. Resilient people are able to look at problems from many different perspectives and take into account lots of different factors when trying to solve them. This gives them far more options.
3. Resilient people are willing to reach out and take risks. They try out new things, believing that failure is a part of life and that life and everything it throws at you is to be embraced. This gives them a certain wisdom.

Anything that helps you cultivate your own resilience is a wise investment.

Perseverance Quick Quiz

Tough times don't last, but tough people do. This is the essence of perseverance. It's what Winston Churchill meant when he famously said: 'Never, never, *never* give up.' How are you, would you say, at staying the course? Bloodymindedness has its place, but it will only get you so far.

Come up with three things that will help you build your perseverance:

1. . . . .

2. . . . .

3. . . . .

Perseverance requires stamina. So what fortifies you and are you making sure there's enough of this in your life?

. . . .

. . . .

. . . .

If you're not making sure there's enough, you're undermining your ability to build your own confidence. So what will give you the strength to go on – and on, and on?

. . . .

. . . .

. . . .

Having a vision so you keep your eye on the bigger game will stop you getting dragged down by temporary local difficulties. So what is the bigger game you wish to be part of?

. . . .

. . . .

. . . .

Having a robust physical and emotional constitution will give you the foundations for enduring success. So what do you need to make sure you're getting enough of?

. . . .

. . . .

. . . .

Confidence key 3: state management

We all have ability. The difference is how we use it.

Stevie Wonder

Ask most people about their *state* and they'll give you a blank look, one that says: 'I haven't a clue what you're talking about.' For lots of people, their state – the way they feel physically and emotionally – is rather like the weather: something they are on the receiving end of, that just happens to them. In this sense, many people live their lives hoping for sunny intervals.

The fact is, your state is not something that just happens to you; it is something you create – and that means you can learn to manage and alter it. To do this, you need first to pay attention to what is going on inside you (your internal state), recognise it and then learn what you can do about it.

Your state is something that continually fluctuates and changes in the course of a single day. It's pretty uncommon to go to bed at night feeling exactly the same as you did when you woke up that morning, so ask yourself: what changed your state during the day?

For most people the answer is: a thousand different things. You get a piece of good news. (Hooray!) Then you rush lunch and get indigestion. (Argh!) You talk to someone you haven't seen for ages. (Aaah!) You hear a favourite piece of music and it reminds you of an old love and you feel nostalgic. (Mmm . . .) Then you get a reprimand from your boss. (Ouch!) You look at your mail and see a letter from the taxman (Ugh!) but then you get a call from a headhunter with news of a job opportunity (Oooh!). And so on. Every one of these represent a change in your state. Put like this, it's a bit of a rollercoaster – no wonder you're tired at the end of the day.

The state you are in at any given moment will either help or hinder you. Remember what it's like to have flu: how you have no energy and feel feverish and weak? This has to be one of the least resourceful states you can be in. Now imagine what it would be like to have to make critical life decisions when in that state – who you will marry, what career to choose, whether to emigrate. Do you think you would be at your best? Possibly not!

If you want to achieve the most you can achieve, you need to be in the best state in order to do so. And that means coming at things in a whole new way. Suppose you want to learn something. A really useful question to ask yourself would be: what state do I need to be in to do this most effectively? Tired, harassed, fearful and defensive probably isn't going to do it – so what would?

This way of thinking is going to be really useful, whatever it is you want to learn. You want to learn a foreign language, improve business performance or have a more fulfilling relationship? Then start by asking yourself: what state do I need to be in to be at my most available to learn? Then ask yourself: so what do I need to do to achieve that state?

You may be surprised by the answers that pop into your head. Trust them. People have quite different ways of getting themselves in the right state and also of refreshing their state periodically. For myself, when I'm writing I will pause every so often and go for a walk so the ideas can sort themselves out. Then, when I get back, the prose flows.

Unfortunately, formal education pays little attention to ascertaining or eliciting optimal learning states. Students of all ages are often given information which, it is presumed, they will then be able to make sense of. But the state they are in prior to that information being given is rarely considered, still less actively enhanced. Imagine how different learning would be if teachers and students actively generated the appropriate states for learning *before* commencing instruction. Well, you can do this for yourself – and NLP anchoring can help you.

You know how a particular song can trigger vivid memories – and feelings – associated with a particular time? That's an anchor. A certain touch makes you feel quite different and every time you're touched in that way you always have that same feeling. That's an anchor, too. Every time you see a particular sight, you always feel the same way. That's another anchor.

The human brain has an amazing ability to connect things so that we have the same associations whenever we re-experience those elements. Some years ago, I was running a programme in a building which had an old-fashioned staff canteen. At lunchtime we'd go down to the canteen and as we went through those swing doors my senses were assailed by the smell of boiled cabbage. Suddenly the memories came rushing back all in an instant. I was back at school, remembering how we had to line up before going into the school hall for lunch; and how there was a thin brown stripe on the wall where we waited; and how we weren't allowed in until the kids from the woodwork room came out – and that meant you waited for their door to open and when it did there was the smell of newly planed wood mingling with the odour of boiled cabbage. All of this from just a smell – that's the power of an anchor!

This incredible associative power can work for us or against us. It's great if every time we hear a certain piece of music we feel inspired and energised, not so great if it reminds us of that time when nothing was going right and we felt like just giving up. Then we may get to experience those feelings all over again.

You're going to find that there are already many anchors in your life and that you yourself are probably an anchor for others. However, you can also create useful anchors for yourself and that's what I want to show you next.

Confidence anchors

Suppose you were to capture every instance of you feeling confident so that you could re-access this state at will. Would that be useful? Then you'll want to create your own Confidence Anchor.

But if you're going to get the most out of such an anchor, you don't just want lots of confident feelings, you also want to capture and be able to re-elicit the knowledge that when things were challenging or unclear or difficult, you were able to stay the course and rise to the challenge. Why? Because knowing you can do this will give you the confidence to do it again and not shy away from the challenges that life presents.

Remember your Confidence Balance Wheel? You're going to want to draw on different areas to establish the most robust kind of Confidence Anchor. So when we start building this anchor, be sure to select from different areas of the Wheel. Before we do this, have a look at your Wheel again and remember some of the episodes from your own life that go with your highest scores.

Once you've created a Confidence Anchor, it would be a really smart move to keep adding to it by firing it off whenever you experience feeling confident. This will strengthen the association between the anchor and the state of confidence you wish to build. Do this and you will rapidly build a powerful resource state that consists of all the times you've ever felt confident. You may also want to add other elements. (What would it be like to have other positive states anchored there too?)

Do this and you will also be teaching your brain to look out for every time you actually are feeling confident. This in itself will be an incredibly helpful thing: you may be pleasantly surprised at how many of these there are. Then you can fire off this anchor whenever you need it and know that it's always becoming more and more robust.

EXERCISE: Creating Your Own Confidence Anchor

We're going to set a physical anchor. To do this, we need a unique stimulus which your brain can associate with confidence. We also want it to be unobtrusive so you can use it pretty much anywhere. Over the past thirty years, NLP practitioners have experimented with many such triggers. Pressing the third finger on your hand against your thumb on the same hand has proven to be the most consistently popular because it's easy and effective. (You choose which hand feels right to you.)

N.B. You only press your finger and thumb together when you're reliving the experiences detailed below. Having relived the experience, release finger and thumb after each step.

1. Think of a time when you were faced with a challenge and you stayed with it – and because you did, you got a good outcome. Step into this experience. Relive this experience as if it was happening right now. Now set your anchor – that is, press your third finger and thumb together. Hold finger and thumb together for as long as this is a strong experience and release while it's still strong – that is, before it begins to fade.

2. Now let's use your Confidence Balance Wheel from Chapter 3. Pick a particular segment. Think of a time when you've felt particularly confident. Relive *this* experience as if it was happening right now. Now set your anchor, pressing third finger and thumb together. Hold finger and thumb together for as long as this is a strong experience and release while it's still strong.

3. Pick a different segment. Think of a time when you've felt particularly confident. Relive *this* experience as if it was happening right now. Now set your anchor, pressing third finger and thumb together. Hold finger and thumb together for as long as this is a strong experience and release while it's still strong.

4. Now, in your mind's eye, put a movie screen up and see a movie of yourself in a situation where you wish to be more confident. Fire your anchor – that is, press third finger and thumb together – and watch how you behave differently.

5. Now, still with your eyes shut, step into that movie with this new state and experience what it's like from the inside. Live the experience at first hand, looking out, as it were, through your own closed eyes.

State management includes both your emotional state and your physical state. And if you think about it, the two are inextricably linked. If you've spent the entire day in front of the computer, trying to meet a looming deadline, then you are likely to end the day in a low energy state. You will be tired from concentrating on the computer screen, your back may be stiff, you may have missed a gloriously sunny day and a quick lunchtime walk to get the job done on time and all this – your emotional and physical state – will directly influence how you experience being alive as you make your weary way home and dream of flopping into bed before you do it all again tomorrow.

The great news is, if you are going to manage your state, then you are going to assume a degree of power and control that most people don't even know is possible. Your first step will be to notice your state and what is going on. Even if you'd like to be feeling differently, your second step is not to try and change your state right now but, instead, pay more attention to it and start to learn more about it. You need to allow yourself to be with your experience. Ask yourself: why am I in this state (emotional, physical or both), what were the triggers, and what could I have done differently to influence my state instead of allowing it to influence me?

You can do this with just about any state you find yourself in. Suppose you are feeling sad and down. Ask yourself: how come? Maybe you are sad due to a loss. It might be the loss of a loved

one. It might be the loss of a job. It may be the loss of a dream –
which is no small thing. Whatever the loss, it is a profound experience. Now you know what you're dealing with. Often this in
itself is a great relief to people, because what they're feeling now
makes sense to them.

So when we start thinking about managing our state, we need
to move into an entirely different way of thinking. It's important
to move at a pace that suits us – no happy-clappy quick fixes or
self-delusion. Let's keep it real. Then we can ask: what other ingredients or resources could I add to change my state? You can think
of this as being just like baking a cake. What do you need to add
to the current mix to get the outcome – more confidence – that
you want? All right, then: think of a time when you've been in that
state and do exactly the same procedure as when creating your
Confidence Anchor – just add this state into the confidence mix.
Relive the experience and anchor it with third finger and thumb.

Suppose you were simply to remember how it feels to be in the
state you want to achieve, whether that is a more relaxed, more
confident, more energetic or more peaceful state. If you want to
be in a more confident state then remember what it feels like,
based on a real experience when you did feel more confident
than you do now. You could just imagine taking that same feeling of sureness and confidence into the new situation you are
facing, one that is a challenge to you and one that will need you
to be in the right state when you embark on it. But you could do
a whole lot more by using the Confidence Anchoring process, as
it will make it more visceral and more real.

You can do this with children, too. Indeed, children have their
own version of this process where they enact possible scenarios;
it's how they learn about the world and what's possible for them.
They call it 'let's pretend'. But here we're doing more than let's
pretend; we're doing 'let's remember' at the same time. Let's
remember what you already have, what you already know how
to do (these are your resources), and let's use these skills in this

new situation where you are not feeling so confident and where they could make all the difference.

Now, suppose you want to feel a certain way and that's going to mean you'll need to change your state, but you've never felt that way before – what do you do then? No problem. Think of someone who is a good role model, who does this way of being really well. What if you don't actually know anyone who embodies this way of being? Which fictional characters have you come across in books, movies or plays who embody this quality or state? Try them on for size. In your imagination, step into that real person or fictional character and be them for a moment or two. Move as they move. Walk as they walk. Talk as they talk. Most importantly, get the feel and as you engage with this experience, notice what this feeling is like because this is the feeling you are going to be taking into your real-life experience. Again, you can do all of this with the anchoring process too.

What you have here can also be thought of as a turbocharged mental rehearsal technique, because it prepares your brain for the challenge ahead. It engenders the right state in you, that is, the confidence to face the upcoming challenge. World-class athletes perform variations on this process all the time. When I'm coaching athletes I find being able to show them actually how to get into the right state to be at their best is incredibly helpful to them.

Preparation is a crucial step in building and maintaining confidence. Too often though, people limit preparation to their material. If you don't *feel* prepared, then you won't feel in control, you're more easily flustered and less likely to feel in command of yourself or the situation.

Feeling prepared is a state in itself. To feel underprepared is to feel under-confident. If you are prepared, you know how you want to feel and you have an anchor you can call on to access this state at will. You have also given some thought to what might happen: you have taken the time and trouble to consider how things might go and, just as importantly, how you want them to go.

You now have the tools to make sure that you are prepared in how you feel in yourself. Now we're ready to look at how you can strengthen your preparedness by using some winning strategies.

Confidence key 4: develop winning strategies

It ain't what you do, it's the way that you do it.

Like the song says, 'It ain't what you do, it's the way that you do it'! A strategy is a sequence of steps that enable you to achieve a goal. Those steps can be mental or physical – or a combination of the two. Very often, these sequences run with amazing rapidity and entirely outside a person's conscious awareness. Let me give you an example.

Many times I have worked with adults and children who lack confidence in their spelling. When I ask them to spell a word they find difficult, their eyes will often go all over the place as they search for the correct spelling. Frequently, a finger or two will go to the mouth as they try to sound out the word, and then they'll look down feeling a bit stupid because they're not sure. By contrast, if I ask a person who consistently spells correctly to spell the same word their eyes will invariably exhibit a quite different and absolutely consistent pattern. They look up and to their left and then read off the word as they see it in their mind's eye. When I ask them if they are sure, they absolutely are because, as one person put it, 'I can see it and it feels right.'

What you have here are two radically different strategies: one works and one doesn't. Whenever someone tells you they don't know how to do something, what they're telling you is that they don't have a successful strategy. This holds true for just about anything, from *I don't know how to do this work task* to *I don't know how to have a long-term loving relationship.*

Over the past thirty years or so, NLP pioneers have spent a lot of time teasing out strategies that really work for all sorts of human activities. These have often been codified into learnable techniques; so yes, there really is an NLP Spelling Strategy, which I have successfully taught to thousands of people.

The more complex the task, the more strategies will probably be involved. Living confidently is more complex than spelling, so there are more elements involved. In a sense, this entire book is designed to give you a confidence strategy, rather like a recipe outlines how to make a dish successfully. You need to get the ingredients together and then follow the steps.

Of course, some strategies work better than others. Some people, for example, may find it difficult to make a decision and this is probably because they have a poor decision-making strategy. Perhaps, when faced with a choice, they mentally seesaw between *on the one hand* and *on the other*, which can end up undermining their confidence. They may end up feeling not just like somebody who cannot make a decision but somebody who is 'too stupid' to make the right choice. They are *not* too stupid. They are simply struggling because they do not have a good decision-making strategy.

By detailing the sequence of steps to follow, strategies provide the 'how to's that people so often lack. One of my coaching clients was an extremely successful executive who had chronic credit-card debt issues. Each month his bill would come and it would be a horrible surprise to him. He was getting pretty depressed, not just about the bills but also about himself because he was losing confidence in his ability to control his finances – and his life. He showed me the statements and I started to ask him about how he came to make the purchases that were shown. After some discussion, it dawned on him that he had a very simple buying strategy which was: 'When I see something I like, if I think it's going to make me feel good I buy it!' That is a strategy all right, but it's one that's almost guaranteed to land you in debt. We needed to install some extra steps. One involved him having a chat with himself about what it would feel like after he'd bought it and the credit-card statement arrived the following month. Another involved him remembering previous impulse-buying decisions and evaluating whether they had really made him feel good for any length of time. (They had not.)

Once he began implementing this new strategy, he was delighted to find that his credit-card bills, in his words, 'miraculously came down'. But there was another, ultimately more important benefit. As our coaching continued, he realised that his buying pattern was actually a decision-making strategy that was running automatically in other areas of his life. He was single and looking for a woman. So when he saw a pretty girl . . . that's right, he'd run the same strategy – or more accurately the strategy would just run and he'd find himself dating all sorts of inappropriate women because he hadn't had that chat with himself about what he was getting into and how did this look in the light of previous impulse buys!

Some years ago, I was working on a project designed to enable salespeople to become more confident about selling a top-of-the-range luxury limousine. I was finding that some of the sales team simply didn't know how to manage the task and that what some of them were secretly struggling with was the fact that the customers who were most likely to buy this type of car left them feeling inadequate. They just weren't used to being around these kinds of people and it undermined their confidence in themselves – so it hit them at the level of Identity. Not what you need if you're seeking to come across as credible.

To get the best results, I needed to know what the successful salespeople did that was different and that worked so well. So I instituted a Confidence Modelling project. Once I was able to give them a sales strategy, based on looking at what it was that the outstanding and more confident salespeople were doing to clinch the deal, their confidence soared and they started to hit their sales targets.

The strategy the outstanding salespeople were using had a very particular sequence and they used it over and over again. It had evolved quite naturally through trial and error. But by teasing it out, it became possible to codify it and then teach it as a set of learnable steps to everyone.

- Walk around the outside of the car with your potential customer. Simply show it to them and allow them to appreciate its visual impact and beauty.
- Invite the client to sit inside the luxury vehicle and go to great pains to adjust the seat to their particular needs so they can experience how comfortable it can be. Show them the various possible adjustments so they can imagine just how smooth and comfortable a ride it can be for them and their passengers.
- Take your customer for a test drive with you behind the wheel. When you reach your destination, switch seats and, on the way back, sit quietly in the passenger seat. Only speak to point out just how quietly the engine runs, the peacefulness of being inside such a luxury car. Allow them to experience this peace and quiet for themselves.

This strategy proved incredibly effective, partly because it addressed *what you see, what you feel* and *what you hear* as a driver. So it's a pretty total experience.

The very best strategies will involve three or more of your senses: what you hear, what you see, what you feel, maybe even what you taste and what you smell. (Some of the car salespeople would also point out the beautiful interior leather and new car smell.) In the New Behaviour Generator, it'll be what you say to yourself (the auditory), what you see (the visual) and what you feel (the kinaesthetic).

EXERCISE: **New Behaviour Generator**

My experience with Confidence Coaching is that the New Behaviour Generator is a particularly useful strategy. It allows you to create new behaviours and mentally try out new ways of being before actually doing them in real life. This test drive allows you to mentally rehearse your new, more confident way of being and so prepare yourself for a different kind of future. This also allows you to make any necessary adjustments.

1. Looking down to your left, ask yourself: 'If I could be more confident, what would that look like?'
2. Having asked yourself this question, look up to your right and see whatever you see. It may be a movie of you behaving or saying something in a particular way; it may just be some blurry colours on that movie screen in your mind's eye. It is whatever it is.
3. Then look down to your right and allow yourself to feel what comes with what was on the screen.
4. Run this sequence at least three times. Each time, take the feeling from step 3 and use that to refashion the statement you make in step 1. So, suppose you see yourself acting more confidently in step 2 and then when you feel how that is in step 3 you say, 'Yes, but I'm not sure that's realistic.' Now when you begin the next iteration your wording will change to, 'If I could be more confident *and* it was realistic, what would *that* look like?'

Keep doing this and the strategy will streamline. That is to say, you'll begin doing it faster and with greater ease. Strategies are a classic demonstration of practice makes perfect. The more you do it, the better you'll get at doing it.

There are numerous refinements we could add to this basic strategy, but if you do this for just five minutes each day on different scenarios it will be like giving your brain – and your imagination – a workout. Little and often is the way to build any kind of muscle – and that goes for your mental muscles, too.

Chapter 5

Confidence in Relationships

Every single relationship you have is affected by confidence. Not just yours, but also that of the other person. Too often, people forget that the other person's confidence is going to play a critical role in the relationship you have with them. Indeed, sometimes what makes all the difference is helping the other person to become more confident, whether that person is an insecure boss or lover. However, our emphasis here is on what you can do to boost *your* confidence.

I'm going to focus on confidence in three particularly important kinds of relationships – your personal, social and sexual relationships. Most people self-score differently in these areas. As always, it's really useful to establish where you already have a fair degree of confidence and where you might like to have more.

Whole books have been written on how to improve relationships. There are so many potential types, from romantic to family, from intimate to mere acquaintances. Our focus here is not going to be on everything to do with relationships, but on how your confidence can be enhanced in certain kinds of relationships.

Knowing you can establish rapport with a wide range of people is fundamental to confident relating. Ultimately, rapport comes from feeling you have been acknowledged and seen. You may think that rapport is natural and spontaneous. That's true, but there are also specific things you can do that will enhance rapport and increase your effectiveness in communicating.

What a person actually says is only one part of the mix. The whole point of being able to establish and maintain rapport is to meet with another person in *their* model of the world so that they feel you have an understanding of where *they're* coming from. The more you can do this, the more you will put them at their ease and the more open they will be to what you have to say.

The better the rapport you have with another, the more likely it is that the message you are sending will be the one they receive. The more this happens, the more you just seem to get on with people – and the more confident you become that this is how it naturally is for you.

To develop this kind of confidence, you'll probably want to know what to pay attention to. Notice how the other person speaks, breathes, gestures and moves. Notice their energy, their characteristic posture, the tone of their voice and their speech patterns. There is a rhythm in all eight of these variables. The more you can match that rhythm, the easier communication will be. Pick one a day to pay attention to – you'll be amazed at how much there is to see, hear and feel.

As you start to notice how people have different speeds (be it of walking or talking, thinking or living), you're going to find it very useful to know about pacing. You have your own natural pace when you walk; other people have theirs. However, when you walk together, you both fall into a shared rhythm. And you do this without any overt negotiation; it just happens. You want the same thing to happen when you're relating to someone else. Getting in sync by paying attention to the variables I listed above will help you do this very quickly.

You will still be you, but hopefully you have enough flexibility to adjust your behaviour. You're really aiming to meet the other person where they're at, while still being you. That way you can enjoy your differences and still feel in sync.

Confidence in Personal Relationships

Of everyone you know, who do you have the most personal relationship with? When I ask clients this question, I get all sorts of answers. You know the answer I get least? 'Myself.'

In fact, you've known yourself longer than you've known anyone else. Whether or not you can remember all of it, you know more about your personal history than anyone else's. And whether you like it or not, you get to hang out with yourself more than with anyone else.

To start building confidence in relating to others personally, we need to begin with the most important relationship you will ever have – your relationship with *you*.

People assume the word relationship only refers to their relationships with others, but the single most important relationship you have is also probably the one you neglect the most. The richer a relationship you can have with yourself, the richer the relationships you'll be able to have with others. The more you know yourself, the more you'll have to share with others.

You can begin paying attention to your relationship with yourself by completing the following exercise.

EXERCISE: Your Relationship with You

Answer these questions truthfully.

What sort of relationship do you have with yourself?
(a) Good.
(b) Bad.
(c) Indifferent.
(d) Never even thought about it.

Do you get on with yourself?
(a) Always.
(b) Sometimes.
(c) Never.
(d) Never even thought about it.

Do you like yourself?
(a) Always.
(b) Sometimes.
(c) Never.
(d) Never even thought about it.

Everything that you might ask about someone else – especially someone you would like to be friends with – you can ask about yourself. Most of the time, people focus their attention externally. Shift your attention now to inside you for a few moments.

How do you relate to yourself? Do you pay attention to your needs? Do you, for instance, make sure that the different bits of you are getting a look in? Do you respect your gut reactions to things, or do you override your instincts and live to regret it? How you engage with yourself is going to affect how you come across to others and also how available you are to engage with them.

Are you, for instance, highly critical of yourself? If you are, how does that make you feel? Would someone want to be your friend if you spoke to them as you do to yourself?

Often this has been a useful starting point for people I've been working with. Simply by adjusting the tone, volume, pitch and location of their internal dialogue, they have started to improve their relationship with themselves. Not only does that internal dialogue sound different, it is very common for these sub-modality changes to actually result in spontaneous changes to the actual content of their dialogue as well. As you can imagine, both then affect how you feel about yourself; you feel more confident. This lets you be more outgoing because you're less afraid of being judged. At the same time, you also become less judgemental of others and so able to enjoy and appreciate a greater variety of different people.

So what's going on here? You still have clear values and standards, but when you start to relate more positively to yourself, you stop beating yourself up; you're no longer disciplining yourself as a stern parent might an errant child. That also means you don't have to find fault with others in this way, either. If you're not blaming yourself, you won't have the same need to blame others to offset the bad feelings you previously created inside yourself.

By adjusting your internal dialogue, you can enjoy major external changes. More confidence means you won't feel so defensive because challenges won't hit you at an Identity level. By contrast, the less confident someone is, the more everything seems like an assault on who they are as a person and the more defensive – which can show up as aggression – they'll become.

By doing this, you're building rapport with yourself. Among the many payoffs when you adopt this new attitude to yourself is that you will start to pay attention more effectively to what is going on with you and you will start trusting your own judgement and wisdom. This, in turn, will give you more confidence in yourself. You will have more confidence that you know what you need to do, too, and you won't then be so dependent on what others think.

This will naturally be a process of trial and error. Over time, you will find you are on the right track more often than not and you will begin to know that you can trust yourself. Your intuition will alert you if you are heading down the wrong path and all you have to do is pay attention.

In a nutshell, it makes a lot of sense to invest time and energy to have a good relationship with yourself. So what would it be like to have yourself over for the evening, the way you would invite a good friend over for supper?

Imagine behaving exactly as you would if it were a friend who was coming over. You would think about what they like to eat and drink. You would make your home warm and welcoming. You would ask them about themselves, give them positive support and encourage their various endeavours. You would want to rally round to help them get back on their feet after a disappointment. You would congratulate them on their achievements and be happy to discuss their hopes and dreams.

Now you already know how to do all these things; but when was the last time you did them for yourself? So what are you doing this evening?

Social Confidence

Gill was used to staying home more than she wanted to. She was used to being lonely. When she thought about going to a social occasion, she would often imagine what it would be like as she arrived. In her mind's eye she would see clusters of people already engaged in animated conversation and laughing. As she imagined approaching them, she would find they didn't notice her. This made her feel small and on the outside. Fearing it would be that way, she would then see what was on television and stay at home. Imagine running this kind of movie for years! That's why Gill contacted me. She lived abroad so we spoke on the phone.

When I asked her about her mind movies they were in full colour, sharply defined and big. Pretty compelling, then. Changing those sub-modalities would certainly make a difference. But what also struck me was that Gill's loneliness was self-inflicted and I wanted her to recognise this. Here's a snippet of the conversation that followed:

Ian: So you fear you'll be ignored?
Gill: Yes – and rejected.
Ian: But who's rejecting who, Gill? By deciding not to go, you reject them before they've even met you!

Gill had never thought of herself as someone who rejected others. That really wasn't part of the movie she was living. The thought stopped her in her tracks. That's why the next thing she did was to hang up!

Later that day, she called me back to say how shocking it was to see herself in this light. Since then, she'd been seeing how this same pattern of pre-emptive rejection showed up in other areas of her life. There were jobs – and men! – she'd not gone for just in case she didn't get them.

Previously, she'd explained things to herself by telling herself she was an introvert, so that meant she'd feel uncomfortable in company. This is a common misperception. Actually she was shy, and that's not the same. You can be an introvert and still have a healthy social life. Introversion does not mean you can't be socially confident. Introverts have a rich inner life and will withdraw to recharge; by contrast, extroverts direct their attention outwards to seek stimulation, which is how they recharge. Both of these styles are perfectly compatible with being socially confident.

Now we could make those sub-modality changes to her movie and get a huge payoff. As we did this, the soundtrack changed too. Previously, part of it was the hubbub of the social scene she was imagining, but part of it was her own inner dialogue where she'd effectively coached herself to get ready to feel bad! Now that had gone and she was delighted.

It seemed to open a door as she started to tell me about times when she had actually gone to an event. Then she'd feel very self-conscious. Her attention was focused on herself rather than on the other people who were there. This meant of course that she really wasn't available to engage with them.

Remember how as an adolescent you could feel really, really self-conscious sometimes? At its worst, self-consciousness can make people feel paralysed and tongue-tied. In all such situations – including public speaking – my advice would be the same. Start paying attention to what's going on out there. Look at people, see their individual features; let your attention be with what they are saying and know that you don't need to have something to say prepared. You just need to be present so that you can respond to what is actually happening in real time. This is so much easier than trying to second-guess what might be said and planning how you might then react.

EXERCISE: Social Confidence Builder

Part 1

1. Be around someone who is socially adept and learn from them. Just hang out with them when they are with other people so that you can see and hear what they say and do. Tell them what you're wanting to achieve. Don't know anyone like this? Really? They don't need to be a superstar, just someone who's got some of what you want.

2. Assemble your dream team from movies and television. Gather clips of people who you see as good role models opening conversations, initiating contact and having interactions. Make your own mental movie of you doing the same thing. Step into the movie and feel it. Tailor it so it fits with you.

3. Set yourself a target of simply speaking to three new people in a safe setting. There is no goal other than that you deliberately initiate contact. This can be a brief interchange or an extended conversation. It doesn't matter; the purpose is to initiate contact.

4. Do this on a regular basis, not just once. Get used to approaching others with no expectations. Do this every day for a week – or the rest of your life. Does this feel like a stretch? Good! Only when you step outside your comfort zone will you be building this new confidence muscle.

Part 2

5. Decide what makes you feel alive and alert. This can be anything. Focus on how you can make this part of your new social connecting routine. For instance:

> **Activities.** Choose three different activities you might or do enjoy. Do them in company and initiate contact with other participants.
>
> **Clothes.** Wear a different colour each day. Notice which colours make you feel at your best and which work best in certain settings. Start wearing what makes you feel alive in the way you want, given the setting.

6. Practise gracefully terminating an interaction. Know that you are free to step away or leave. Again, look to your role models, real or celluloid, for demonstrations of how to do this. Have an exit strategy. You may even want to have an excuse ready that you can use.

Social Competence Builds Social Confidence

Do you feel nervous approaching or starting a conversation with people you don't know, or just awkward in social situations generally? Then it's going to be useful to know how to conduct yourself – and this means learning certain behaviours which, when combined, constitute a social skill set.

To develop these skills, you will need to do two things: invest time in developing them, and then keep practising them. Then all you need to do is keep doing them for the rest of your life! Yes, really, the rest of your life. Why? You know from your own experience that even if you're good at something, the more you do it the better you can become. Too often people imagine that once they're socially confident, that'll be that. In fact, the skill requires ongoing practice through repeated exposure to social situations, because what you don't use you lose. Even the very socially confident need to keep their hand in!

Here's what you'll need to do:

1. **Create social opportunities**. That means first stop avoiding social situations and stop turning down social invitations. Then start suggesting outings with people you want to know better and start inviting people over.
2. **Pay attention to non-verbal communication**. People are continually signalling unconsciously whether they want more or less. Pay attention to their physical expressions, be they facial or full body. Take an NLP training course in Rapport Building to get good at this.
3. **Practise your own body language**. If you're stooped and stuttering and busy avoiding eye contact, you'll probably come across as anxious and make others nervous too. On the other hand, you'll come across as more open if you smile, nod with

interest and lean in towards a person, even as you have easy eye contact. (Focusing around the eyes as well as looking directly at them is quite sufficient. You don't want eyeball-to-eyeball staring matches!)

4. **Be more interested in the other person than in how you're coming across.** Paying attention is one of the greatest compliments you can pay another human being. Show you're paying attention with brief conversational encouragers – nodding, smiling, interjections like 'Really?', 'Uh huh' and so on.

5. **Develop your emotional intelligence.** To understand what's going on for others you need to be able to read them emotionally. It's much easier to make sense of other's emotions when you can make sense of your own. This is where many people, especially men, have a blind spot. Again, this is why developing that relationship with yourself is so important. You can do this on your own or with additional coaching input.

6. **Engage in active listening.** Ask people questions about themselves, such as their views, what they enjoy doing and significant events in their life. Go for what captures your interest. This will make it very likely that, should you meet them again, you'll be able to make reference to what they were talking about. ('*How nice that someone remembered.*') Now you've got social continuity, too.

7. **Don't take lack of response as a personal insult**. Some people will just not be available when you are. They may be preoccupied, too busy running their own agenda, out of sorts or just shy. Get back in the game and go talk to someone else *now*.

Sexual Confidence

Sexual confidence is not just an issue for young adults or those in the dating game. The lack of it can show up in all sorts of ways and at any age. To take just two examples: many older women have told me that they've started to feel invisible – as if they are no longer seen as sexual at all by our society. Not surprisingly, this really knocks their confidence. And many men and women – even those in long-term relationships – have told me how they are afraid to say what they really want from their partner.

But it doesn't have to be this way. Having worked with thousands of people, I'd like to share with you what has made a real difference to people's sexual confidence, whatever their age. I want to focus on three areas, each of which has its challenges: how you can be more sexually confident just in yourself; how you can be more sexually confident at the beginning of a possible new relationship; and how to be sexually confident in an ongoing relationship.

You in yourself

You will almost certainly at some point in your life have encountered someone who seems to have sexual allure but doesn't fit into the usual stereotypes of what is sexy. This is the man or woman who walks into a room and seems to attract attention without even trying. Invariably, they are comfortable in their own skin and self-assured. This gives them a certain confidence – and *this* makes them sexually attractive.

Once again, how you are in yourself and how you are with yourself is potentially going to make a big difference in how you come across. So everything we've been focusing on so far can contribute to that aura of self-confidence which is potentially sexually attractive.

Ultimately your sexual attractiveness is not dependent upon you being the right height, the right weight, the right size, the right shape or the right age. These things can certainly affect how *you* feel about yourself and they may need addressing – particularly if they show up in disparaging and critical internal dialogue or catastrophic mental movies in which the world trashes you.

Use the tools we've already been working with to address these. (see page 66 for internal dialogue and page 67 for changing your mental movies). Also be sure to challenge the assumptions contained in both by using the ABC model (see page 78). But for the rest of the world, achieving the Photoshop version of you is not as important as you may have thought. If this really was the be all and end all, those people who don't fit into the stereotypes wouldn't be able to turn heads as they do.

Getting rid of the negatives is one thing. In addition, there are some things you can do which are going to positively enhance your sexual confidence. Suppose you'd never really learnt how to drive and then you were given a car and expected to drive it: just how confident would you feel, especially if someone was going to be in the car with you? It's not that different with your own body or someone else's. Do you know how to drive it? This is why self-pleasuring is so important, especially for women. When you know what works for you, you also know how you work. Taking the mystery out of how you experience intense pleasure and reach orgasm is going to give you more confidence. It also means you can teach your partner what's best for you. By all means read some manuals, but make sure you road test what works for you.

Ask men or women, gay or straight, what they find most attractive about another person and they will invariably cite confidence as one of the key factors. People often don't realise what this means. Very simply, confidence is an aphrodisiac! Whatever investment of time, money and attention you make in becoming more confident can potentially have a sexual payoff, too, because you feel differently about yourself and come across differently. Of course, when you come across as at ease with your sexuality and comfortable in your own body you will definitely appear sexually confident.

So *are* you at ease with your sexuality and comfortable in your own body? Being at ease with your sexuality covers everything from sexual orientation to what turns you on. Are you able to relax and enjoy sex, or are you held back by certain inhibitions?

If so, you may want to explore and unpack these with a trusted friend or a professional rather than trying to ignore them.

Anything you can do to make you feel more comfortable in your body is going to be very good news. One woman I worked with found regular yoga classes made her more supple. It wasn't that she wanted to be able to do every position in the *Kama Sutra*; she just felt stiff in social settings and that made her feel awkward. The yoga made her relax and that affected how she carried herself. She stopped feeling so uptight and that made her movement – and her conversation – more fluid. Men responded differently to her because her movement patterns had changed. One man who'd known her before and after she started the yoga said she seemed less formal and less intimidating. I saw a similar kind of change happen with a man I was coaching, who spent a lot of time looking down at the floor. He'd got into that habit at one time in his life when he was feeling pretty down, and although he was now over that, he'd forgotten to update his behaviour. When we practised how it would be for him to walk around looking up and meeting people's gaze, he said he felt like a different person. He certainly looked entirely different and the messages his body was giving off told a very different story. Significantly, within a week he'd started dating a woman.

Starting a new sexual relationship

Many people experience what is really an intense form of performance anxiety when beginning a sexual relationship. For some, it's the first time of having sex with a new partner that is the most stressful. One client, Bill, who was thirty-five, described how he would feel like he was an adolescent again, with sweaty palms and a racing heart. Once the first time was over, he was fine but there was this great – self-imposed – hurdle to overcome first. Luckily, his libido was strong enough to ensure he didn't retreat into celibacy. What lay behind all this stress was that he'd convinced himself that any possible future for the relationship depended on 'how well he did' and proving that he 'could make her feel really good'.

Essentially he had to prove that he could deliver if he was to stand a chance of having a relationship. When I asked him how he thought it was for her, he said he'd never really thought about it from her point of view. Using a particular technique I'm going to show you in a minute, I suggested he step into her shoes and experience how it was for her dealing with him. He found it revealing and said that as her, he'd felt anxious and 'done to: there's not much for me to do as he goes through his moves to prove his mettle'.

When he checked this out with a woman he'd had a short relationship with, she confirmed what he'd said but added that she felt kind of left out. She said she would have liked them to have got to know each other. For her, the sign of a really confident man was that he was in no hurry and he didn't have anything to prove. That was what made her relax.

This was pretty shocking for Bill: his strategy for winning approval was actually turning women off and making it harder to establish a basis for an ongoing relationship. So often, people feel that the other person just doesn't get it. They'll even say things like: 'How do you think it is for me?' But until you have a way of actually stepping into their experience, you won't really know. That's why this next technique is so useful. This is not just a pen and paper exercise; for this you really do want to move around, not least so that you can literally get a different perspective on things.

EXERCISE: Trading Places

1. Find a space, step into it and describe what you're thinking and feeling – just the headlines – as you imagine beginning to engage sexually with your partner.

2. Step out of that space and clear your head by moving around for a few moments

3. Step into a second different physical space and imagine being your partner. As your partner, say what you're thinking and feeling – and hoping.

4. Now step out of that space also, clear your head and have a look at the two spaces from a different vantage point. What strikes you about these two people? What does the one who is you need to do next to make things easy for both of them?

5. See that happening in your mind's eye and notice how the other responds.

6. Step into that same space where the other was before and, as them, experience how it feels to have you acting in this different way.

7. Come back to your original space, be you and again experience the difference.

Sexual confidence in an ongoing relationship

So you've been together some time. Is it still as good as it was? Even if it is, it won't be the same, because relationships mature. If you're lucky, you'll go from falling in love to being in love to loving deeply. And all the while you can become more sexually confident, as long as you're both clear that you're having a relationship, not giving a performance.

An ongoing relationship can be one of the best places to build sexual confidence – but only if both of you can be spontaneous, adventurous, open, playful and caring. Think about it: where do most men and women get their sexual self-assurance from? Why, from their partners of course. So anything that you can do to give yours more self-confidence is going to do you both a lot of good and lead to some very good times.

There are so many things you can do to build the sexual

self-confidence of both of you that I thought I'd include a Top 10 list based on what I've seen make a significant difference. One caveat: this Top 10 is in no particular order – only you can decide what the order should be. See which of these resonate with you and then talk them through together.

Sexual Confidence Top 10

- **First, you need to leave your headspace.** Whether you're idealising the other or trying to play the whole interaction as a game and figure out what slick tricks will get the desired result, you're in your head. That means you're not really present in your body. And that means you're not available to respond easily and fully to what you actually experience. Being real is a sexual attractor in its own right because it indicates you are confident enough to be yourself.

- **Learn how to give pleasure.** A lot of men lack confidence in their ability to give a women intense and sustained pleasure. Many women are not sure what works best for a man. Learning will only happen if you pay attention to the responses you're eliciting. All of these will be informative – even the ones that may suggest you're going in the wrong direction.

- **See responses as feedback not failure.** If your partner doesn't get as turned on as you hoped, that just means something else is needed; it may be something completely different, or what you're doing in a different way, or what you're doing plus something else. Just ask. And from the other side, don't be afraid to encourage, request or even tell.

- **Relax! Take your time.** Stop going for instant results. Sex is one place where instant gratification is unlikely. It's also disappointing compared to what's possible if you let it build.

Feeling some kind of hurry-up time pressure will also often stop whatever response is building in its tracks stone cold, especially in a woman.

- **Reframe rejection fears.** People are particularly susceptible to feeling rejected if they believe they've been rebuffed sexually. It's because our sexuality is so closely associated with our sense of self. So suddenly you're dealing with an Identity level issue. Get your identity off the line and get ready to learn at a Capability level *how to* engage and please this person.

- **Stop hoping this person will be perfect: they won't be.** Idealisation is the enemy of intimacy and connection – but also of sexual spontaneity. Just because they turn out to be human doesn't mean you can't have a good time. Ultimately you'll have a more satisfying relationship because you're having it with a real person. Why? Because you'll have permission to be real, too.

- **Be physically affectionate outside the bedroom.** Too often men can forget that touch is important outside of sex. Non-erotic physical affection sends a message that you are cherished for yourself. This is affirming at an Identity level. The more a person feels affirmed, the more open they can be and the more available they can be. So, paradoxically, non-erotic physical affection from your partner can end up making you feel more sexually available.

- **Keep sex in perspective.** Unless you're planning a life of one-night stands, sex is going to be part of some kind of ongoing relationship. So where does it fit? Is it the most important thing in your relationship? Is it why you're together? Is it why you stay together? When I ask people this, it's striking how few people say yes. So what's the package that sex is part of?

- **Sex is glue.** Just because it's part of a bigger package doesn't mean it isn't important. Go too long without being sexual with each other and the relationship suffers, so get clear about how long is too long and agree about how often is ideal for each of you. I've worked with couples where the most significant enhancement to their sex life was to agree to have sex every so many days, regardless of whether they particularly felt like it or not. It brought them closer together and made them both more sexually confident.

- **Let sex evolve.** There are going to be certain ways of having sex that you'll really love – and you'll always want them to be part of the mix. But what else might you add in? Anything you hanker for? It may be something obviously sexual, but not necessarily. Many women, for instance, just want their men to talk more. The more communication there is, the more comfortable and confident in the relationship she can feel, then the safer it is to let go sexually.

And Finally . . .

Having looked at what you can do to enhance both your confidence and your relationships, it's worth remembering that you will not get on with everyone all of the time. If you really want to have better relationships, you'll need to have the confidence to say, 'You do you and I'll do me.' That way you will become someone who has something money cannot buy: integrity.

That's something else confidence can give you: the ability to stand your ground and be yourself. Then you get to have people in your life who value you for who you are.

Chapter 6

Confidence in the Workplace

Veteran pilot Chesley 'Sully' Sullenberger became a hero in the flash of a New York minute in 2009 when he safely landed US Airways Flight 1549 in the Hudson River, saving 155 lives. Sullenberger, in his late fifties, always maintained that he was just doing his job, but the cool-headed actions of the former fighter pilot and his crew were hailed as an amazing act of *confidence* and bravery by the media.

The outcome of the incident – which was potentially horrific after both engines became disabled following a mid-air collision with a flock of Canada geese – hinged solely on the pilot's confidence in himself and his crew. Interviewed about the crash landing, Captain Sullenberger told reporters: 'I was sure I could do it.'

Sullenberger's thought process surrounding the emergency is instructive. When asked by a reporter if he panicked he said no and talked instead of 'a startle factor' because his first response was simple disbelief. His recovery time, however, was fast so that within a few seconds he began dealing with the challenge at hand. While some of the passengers later said they thought they were going to die, he had remained calm and confident that a safe landing could be made on water without the plane breaking up. Although in a serious situation he had never before faced, the pilot used his previous flight experience to execute a miraculous landing:

> I knew the fundamental things I would have to do, and I was confident that I could do them. I knew I had to focus on the flight path, keep the airplane from hitting too hard, keep the wings level, have the nose up.

Instead of being overwhelmed, Captain Sullenberger had in his mind a series of specific tasks he needed to execute successfully. But that wasn't all.

His confidence and commitment to deliver came not just from being good at his job but also from his values – and these were formed partly by apparently unrelated life events and the meaning he made of them. In the book *Highest Duty: My Search for What Really Matters,* he makes it clear that he sees his entire life as bringing him to that point. He was prepared because he had lived his life in what he called 'a thoughtful way.' In particular his father's suicide and his inability to prevent it had a profound effect on how he viewed life. Life became extraordinarily fragile, fleeting and precious. Gradually, in the wake of this traumatic experience, he came to hope that through a series of small actions over the course of his life he would be able to know that his being here would have made a difference.

This is the backstory to a major news event. In those critical moments on that particular morning above the Hudson the fact that he had not been able to save his father made him all the more anxious to save as many lives as possible.

If you want to understand why he was so good at what he did, you need to take into account how Sullenberger's beliefs and values meant he was totally motivated to deliver – in this case, life itself. He had taken something from a very tough time and made something of it that enhanced how he lived and motivated him to do things to the best of his ability.

Confidence is often a mix of what you can do and what you believe. Having the skills is only part of the story. Certain values and beliefs will prove a powerful motivator for excellence. While these may produce positive results, they may have been born out of anything but positive life experiences. In a sense you could say those passengers owe their lives not to Sullenberger's father committing suicide but to how he reacted to it.

This is an extreme example of a really important principle: it's often not so much what has happened to you but what you make of it that is going to be the deciding factor in whether an experience can strengthen or undermine your confidence. And this is true in every life, even when there's nothing as dramatic as a landing on water. That's why some years ago I invented the Confidence Resumé.

Your Confidence Resumé

Professionally a resumé is a tailored review of what you have done and accomplished to this point. Every successful resumé is never just a list of dates: it is also a narrative which shows how your past experience relates to the new position you're applying for. It's your opportunity to show how your previous experience would be an asset and why an employer should give your application serious consideration.

Your Confidence Resumé, however, is for your eyes only. It's a way of taking stock and reviewing what you can bring to the table. My clients have found it a really useful process.

EXERCISE: Compiling Your Confidence Resumé

Just look back over time and reflect on your past achievements – any and all: from winning the egg-and-spoon race when you were four to major adult achievements both inside and outside work. Start with some basic questions: where, in the past, did you excel? Where – and be honest with yourself – were you not so hot and how have those experiences contributed to where you are now?

You can approach and build your Confidence Resumé in whatever way you prefer. You might want to split it up into decades of your life and ask yourself, for each of those decades, what were the confident highs and the not-so-confident lows? What were the confidence-boosting ups and the confidence-draining downers?

As you review the past, look out for events – good or bad – that have shaped your way of thinking, your beliefs and your values, so that you can take stock of these too. As with Sullenberger, you may find some surprising connections. Often these will have had an impact on your confidence, how you conduct yourself and what you believe is possible. The more of your life you can bring to work, the more you will have to draw on professionally.

- What have you excelled at?
- Where were you not so hot?
- What have been your confidence highs?
- What have been your confidence lows?
- What key life events involving you and others would you include?
- What are the lessons you draw from this?
- List five achievements that made you feel good about yourself.
- How has your confidence changed over time?
- What do you have going for you right now?
- What new opportunities are opening up for you?

- How does your life experience so far equip you for these new opportunities?

Your resumé should include what you think is good, not what other people think or tell you is noteworthy or great.

As you read through your greatest hits and those key events, imagine yourself experiencing the same things again. What would you do differently this time? How would you apply things you know now, which you didn't know back then?

Many people report that when they go through this process, it feels like they're gathering all the pieces of their life together for the first time. If you feel there are many disparate things, that's fine. Too many people leave their treasures scattered on the beach. The more scattered you feel, the less confident you feel. Instead, I want you to gather them up so that you can see what's in your treasure chest.

Confidence in Your Presentation Skills

Being able to speak in public is essential if you are to have professional confidence. However, fear of public speaking is far and away the most common fear that Confidence Coaches deal with. Many people hide behind PowerPoint presentations: these then become little more than tedious data dumps. But the art of presenting is to engage with your audience. That means they need to have a sense of you as a person and what you stand for.

If people don't believe in you as a presenter, your presentation won't have any credibility. It's much easier to believe in a presenter when you have some sense of what they believe. You know what someone believes not just by what they say but also by what they do. How you behave is going to be crucial if you are to be credible.

So what affects the way you behave when presenting? There are some obvious things that will affect how you come across. The most obvious is the one I often hear first when I ask people: 'I need to feel that I know my stuff . . . that I'm in command of my material . . . that I'm on top of my subject.' What most people don't realise is that this isn't just about knowing your stuff – that's not enough; it's about feeling that you know it. So the way you feel – that is, your state – is going to be crucial to how confidently you come across. This is why it's one of the Four Confidence Keys. It's therefore going to be really important to know how you are going to get into the right state come the moment. For many people, the process is all a bit hit and miss; they just hope it'll be all right on the night. This is a high-risk strategy!

Getting clear about the appropriate state and how to be in it is the missing piece in so many people's preparation for a presentation. And it's not just the presenter's state that often doesn't get much attention before the event. Equally important is the question: what state does the audience (be it of one or 10,000) need to be in to be able to get what you're saying? The skilled presenter knows it's his job to make sure the audience is in that state. He therefore has to figure out what he could do that will bring this about. Is there a particular activity or anecdote that will have the desired effect?

There's an old NLP saying: you cannot *not* influence other people. Just by being in a room with another person you will have some impact on them, even if you don't open your mouth – sometimes especially if you don't open your mouth. The same holds true with presenting. Whatever you do, you most certainly will have an effect on other people's states. Whether it's a useful one is quite another matter. Even the most boring one-hour after-lunch PowerPoint presentation will certainly have an effect. (It can be very restful!)

I was once consulting to the board of one of the big advertising firms about how they could pitch more effectively to would-be clients. This was a red-hot team of five who were brimming with ideas but frustrated by their conversion rate. I asked them to give me a demonstration of what they were proposing to do at a presentation later in the week. The lead was taken by an extremely qualified woman who outlined to me, posing as a potential client, what they had to offer.

After a few minutes, I stopped the presentation and asked her how she felt in herself. 'Tight' was her reply. That made sense, as I could hear it in her voice. So far she had been presenting sitting down. I invited her to get up and walk and talk. As soon as she began to walk her voice started to change. Now the pent-up energy had some place to go. Her throat eased and she became more fluent. Within a few minutes she had found her pace both for walking and talking. Now she was comfortable in herself. I asked her to pause and notice the difference. 'I feel more like myself and I can think more clearly,' she replied. I too felt different: I was more engaged and more alert. The way she was in herself was affecting how I was – and this was just a role play.

Next I asked her why this pitch mattered to her. She was very clear about this: 'It would open the door for us. If we can show we can deliver for the business, my whole team would then be able to pitch for work with the charitable arm of their business. That's what I'd really like.' This was news to her other board members and it made immediate sense to them. Suddenly a different kind of energy was being released, the emotional energy that comes with passion. She really cared about this.

So if you want to be more confident when presenting, you need to mobilise both your physical energy but also your emotional energy. You need to care enough to be passionate. When you care, they'll be interested.

One other thing which is going to make a big difference is how you actually look and see your audience. Too often people feel intimidated and so try to minimise contact with their audience.

This is just about the worst thing you can do. People interpret this behaviour as showing that you're unsure of yourself or what you're saying (and so maybe they should be too?), or they think you're aloof or even shifty. Instead, presenters need to remember that any audience is made up of individuals who have their own concerns and private lives. Instead of seeing a group of people as just one intimidating mass of judges, actually look at these people and see their individual faces and features. Let them be people again and start relating to them as such. Give them back their humanity and they'll give you back yours.

Presentation Confidence Boosters

1. **Prepare ahead of time by thinking in terms of states.**
   (a) Ask yourself: what state do you want these people to be in so that they can be at their most receptive?
   (b) Decide how you could elicit this state in them. Is there a story or an activity that will do this?
   (c) Ask yourself: what state do *you* need to be in to do this?
   (d) Decide how you will elicit this state in yourself.
   (e) Ask yourself: what state do you want your audience to be in at the end of your presentation?
   (f) Decide what *you* need to do to make this possible.
2. **Mobilise your physical energy to energise you and your audience.** Use your Confidence Anchor (see page 91) to get you in the best state. Also, remember that so many people fall into the trap of staying static while presenting. The less mobile you are, the less energised your voice and demeanour will be. Get up and move around.
3. **Mobilise your emotional energy to energise you and your audience.** Release your passion, if you don't care why

should they? And, if what you're presenting really doesn't grab you, ask yourself: is it time to be moving on?

4. **Give your audience back their humanity.** Presenters frequently intimidate themselves by viewing their audience – especially if it is a sizeable one to them – as one amorphous mass. Look again and see the individual people who make up your audience. Look at their faces, let them be individuals again and connect with them. Then you won't feel overwhelmed.

Confident Decision-making

It could be said that Captain Sullenberger is a person who knows about confident decision making. It is striking to me how in every interview he consistently demonstrated what I call 'the language of confidence'. This is a way of expressing competency and true confidence without being bombastic. He says that he was confident he could make the emergency landing and keep the plane (and its passengers) intact because he was confident he knew the fundamentals and that allowed him to make a series of decisions that saved all those lives.

The language we use affects how we come across to others. If you want to make a confident impression and instil confidence in those people who are affected by your decisions, you need to pay attention to your language and what it's conveying to others. To take the extremes, are you sounding more tentative and timid than you feel or are you in danger of coming across as bombastic?

Most people have never really thought about it, or just open their mouth and, well, who knows what's going to come out. But anyone can master appropriately confident language usage. I say this from experience: on one occasion I was running a programme focusing on confident language. While most people were finding better ways of expressing themselves and carrying others with them, one delegate found the whole idea quite baffling and couldn't see the point of crafting her language. We then did a role play which featured her and her boss, who she found a little intimidating. By changing her language she began to feel more confident and able to stand her ground. She was pleased and so was I. But I knew that this impeccably dressed woman had really got it when I overheard her telling one of her colleagues during the break that 'choosing the right language is just as important as choosing the right dress'!

This is where the Confidence Language Continuum comes in. It's a way of helping you determine how your language positions you at the moment.

The Confidence Language Continuum

Where would you put your choice of language on this continuum?

Timid . . . Tentative . . . CONFIDENT . . . Over confident . . . Bombastic

Do you consistently use words or phrases which sound timid or tentative to others? This can include constantly asking others *What do you think?* and being too unsure to venture an opinion of your own. *Do you think we should . . . ? Perhaps . . . ? Maybe . . . ? Should we . . . ?* are all language patterns that indicate someone who is tentative about making a decision.

Confident decision-making requires a degree of ownership of a suggestion, idea or proposal using confidence-inspiring words and phrases like: *I think we might want to . . . How about we . . . ? I was thinking it would be good if we could . . . ? What if we were to . . . ?* The hallmark of confident decision-making is that it remains a dialogue between all the parties involved and allows for plenty of flexibility and more than one opinion.

Overconfident decision-making can be as unsettling to others as timid or tentative non-decision-making. Overconfidence is really a misplaced confidence about how things will work out and, perhaps, an overconfidence in your own judgement. Notice, when Sullenberger is talking about his decision-making, he does not come across as overconfident (things are bound to work out when I crash land on the river) or as bombastic (my way or no way). His is a true confidence based on due diligence; he has gathered the information he needs to make his decision (the engines have failed; the craft is high enough to cruise over and clear the Washington Bridge) and he has listened to additional information from air traffic controllers.

When you are looking at your own language of confidence, ask yourself:

- Do I need to turn it up?
- Do I need to turn it down?
- Am I, like Captain Sullenberger, in just the right place?

Build your confidence through chunking

There's something else we can glean from Sullenberger's description of his experience. I was fascinated when I read in an interview with him that he was *not* confident he could solve *all* the problems he and his crew were facing once the plane's engines had failed, but he *was* confident he could solve the next one.

In other words, he did not become overwhelmed by the enormous challenge of the bigger picture – a safe landing with no loss of lives – but tackled each challenge as it arose. This is the art of chunking: taking any challenge and breaking it down into manageable chunks. It is one of the most important tools available to you.

Any time you feel inadequate or overwhelmed, ask yourself how you can break the challenge down into manageable chunks. Do this enough and, as Sullenberger demonstrated, you can avoid being overwhelmed even when there are only minutes to impact.

EXERCISE: Confidence Chunking

1. Think of an issue that seems *big*. It may be current or one from the past.

2. Imagine being able to tackle it because there are a series of steps to success and you have time to do them one at a time.

3. Determine what would be the best sequence to do those steps in.

4. In your mind's eye, run a movie of you doing the steps one after the other over whatever time period is needed and see how it looks from the outside. Make any useful adjustments that occur to you as you watch the movie.

5. Now speed the movie up so you see the complete sequence. Experiment with different speeds.

6. Step into the movie and experience what it's like to take each step one at a time but quite rapidly. Make any useful adjustments.

7. Run this experience again with you living it and, bringing third finger and thumb together, add this to your Confidence Anchor.

Confident Collaboration

The most successful leaders are invariably collaborators. They know they can't do it all on their own. That means they need to work effectively with others. Some of the biggest decisions you will need to make at work – and make with confidence – will revolve around collaboration.

Ultimately collaboration comes down to trust. Can you trust those you're working with? That raises a whole bunch of questions at lots of different Logical Levels. Can you trust their honesty and integrity (Identity); their judgement (Belief); their skill level (Capability); and can you trust them to deliver in particular circumstances (Behaviour and Environment)?

Over twenty years ago, I founded an organisation called International Teaching Seminars. It has gone from strength to strength and is now recognised as the most successful NLP and coaching organisation in the world. I had the vision and I am the founder, but the reason it is still going strong today is that there is a team running it. The people I work with, I work *with*. They have an amazing collaborative spirit, they'll cover for each other, argue vigorously with each other – and me! (I often tell clients that this kind of confidence would make a lot of organisations much more energised.) If I look at my own evolution over these years, I would say that one of the great lessons for me has been not only to delegate more but also to trust more. I think I've done it in stages, when it felt safe because they understood what I was trying to achieve and I saw them deliver.

Confident collaboration leads to *smarter* working. Nobody works in a bubble; knowing how to work with other people is a skill you will be able to apply in every job and every workplace you land in. We saw in Chapter 2 how there are many different types of confidence; the same applies to collaboration. There are as many different potential types of collaboration as there are types of relationships. But confident collaboration needs to be realistic.

EXERCISE: Recognising Confident Collaboration

Have a look at the list and see if the different one-line descriptions fit anyone you've been professionally involved with.

- Your collaborator is overconfident in you and under-confident in themselves.
- Your collaborator is overconfident in themselves and under-confident in you.

- Your collaborator is overconfident in you and in themselves (deluded!).
- Your collaborator is under-confident in you and under-confident in themselves.
- Your collaborator is confident in you and confident in themselves.

A good collaboration demands confidence or trust between all the parties involved, so before you agree to work together, ask yourself: do you feel the other parties have confidence in you and do *you* have confidence in you? If you are seeking smarter collaboration, you will also have to check that you and those you plan to collaborate with have a strong sense of shared values and can trust both each other's work and expertise.

You can attempt any number of collaborations that look good on paper, but if you don't share the same values then you are unlikely to succeed. From a sense of shared values a shared vision will emerge, together with the conviction that what you can achieve together is better than what you can achieve alone. Collaboration is always best when all the parties involved are coming to the project from a position of strength, and that must include you. So ask yourself: are you confident you have something of value to contribute?

Confident collaboration: a case history

Maggie and Julia first met working on a local newspaper, where Maggie was the senior reporter, by ten years, and Julia the newbie on the news beat. Maggie took the younger Julia under her wing and made sure she was not 'exposed' in any way while she got to grips with the workplace, the new characters who were her editors there and a tougher, more tabloid way of working than she was used to.

That was twenty years ago. Today, Julia and Maggie still collaborate on work projects. Only now, Julia, as a magazine editor, calls the shots and Maggie, as a freelance features writer, responds. Maggie, my client, told me she loved working with Julia because: 'She knows what she wants, which makes it easier for me to deliver. I get great briefs and she always remembers to say thank you, which is practically unheard of in journalism these days.'

What this relationship demonstrates is that the very best collaborations are not static, but can and will change over time. Julia is very good at what she does and Maggie knows that. Maggie is very good at what she does and Julia knows that too. This is an excellent collaborative relationship and likely to last until one or both of them retire!

From fear to collaboration

Two of the most common telltale signs of a lack of professional confidence are people being 'super-procedural' and doing every little thing by the book, or constructing elaborate paper trails designed to absolve them of any responsibility should an initiative fail. Colleagues who are covering their backs are driven by fear, which is the absolute opposite of confident collaboration and behaviour. When you have true confidence, you are willing to take responsibility and be accountable, whatever the outcome of the collaboration.

Not long ago, I was working with a recently appointed schools superintendent in the United States, who was based in an up-and-coming district. He'd got this great job, but, to his surprise, he was now feeling unsure of himself and how to proceed. He was concerned there just didn't seem to be what he termed 'a spirit of collaboration'. As we talked, I asked him about his predecessor, who had left under something of a cloud. I suggested he talk privately with some of his key staff to get a sense of what it had been like to work for this man. It turned out that he had been something of a bully and fostered a culture of fear.

Bullies hate collaboration because it is empowering. Bullying comes from a presupposition that you can only have leverage if others are afraid. Of course, what this means is that the bullies come from a place of fear: they're afraid that if you're not afraid, they won't be able to hold their own.

Sure enough, teachers in these schools had learned not to be proactive but to ensure someone else signed off on any initiative so it wasn't going to rebound on them at some later date. The result was an ever-wary and isolated mindset and an eagerness not to be held accountable. To be accountable would be to put yourself in the bully's firing line. So my client's predecessor had effectively undermined the confidence of the teaching staff – who were then supposed to build the confidence of their students! However, as I pointed out to him, by undermining the confidence of the teachers, something else had happened systemically which was a real paradox: on the one hand, this was a school system where students were supposed to be learning, but the school system itself was not a learning organisation.

What to do? The next step was to look at how he might change this culture. Trust and transparency became the watchwords. The most important thing he – or anyone – could do to foster collaboration was to begin acting in a trustworthy and a trusting way. You signal you are going to trust when you begin trusting others with something that matters to you, so he needed to disclose something of himself and what he was about, especially his beliefs and values.

Asking for their help, consulting with them and then taking clear decisions would signal things were going to be different. Making clear commitments and delivering – that is, holding himself accountable – was the best way to begin showing what he expected of them. Rewarding collaborative initiatives by giving them prominence and funding and then giving his staff credit would also be a radical departure and send a strong message. As we continued to explore possibilities, he realised there were so many things he could do which would really be him just starting to function in the way he felt most comfortable anyway. In the process, he would be modelling a completely different leadership style from that of his predecessor. This would put him at ease and allow him to give of his best. It would also mark a radical break with the past. Just fleshing out these possibilities enabled him to regain his confidence. Starting to put these ideas into action resulted in the teachers coming back to life. The atmosphere changed, and student grades improved too.

More confident meetings

The best meetings invariably involve some degree of collaboration and that's going to require trust. If you want to enhance trust, you're going to want to get clear ahead of time what you and the other parties are going for. The more you're ready in yourself for a meeting, the more confident you will be. Stepping into the shoes of the other parties is one of the most useful things you can do to achieve this. We've already seen how you can do this at a practical level with personal relationships (see Trading Places, page 115). Now let me show you a way of applying the same principle to getting ready for any significant meeting.

Remember that you are working with your 'version' of the other person or the other team. To get a better understanding of them, you need to do your best to step into their shoes. This doesn't mean, of course, you will absolutely know what is going through the other person's head, but you will get a better feel for what they may be thinking and then you can work to your best guess. In this way you can save time and generate new ideas about where to go when you actually have the meeting.

I have taught this process to individuals and teams at every level of seniority. Sometimes I have had people physicalise each position so that they literally step into a different space for each point of view. (This seems to be most effective.) Other times people have sat with a piece of paper and just imagined moving around. Both ways, people invariably tell me that they are surprised by how quickly it works, how informative it is and how they feel more prepared – and hence more confident.

EXERCISE: How to Have More Confident Meetings

In simple terms, if you want more effective meetings and better relationships, you need to get clear why the other people are coming to a meeting and what it is they want. This exercise is an incredibly effective way of doing this. When you step into someone else's shoes, you feel like you have a better sense of them and that means you can relate to them personally and professionally with more confidence.

Set out three different spaces on the floor, numbered one to three. Each will have a different function and afford you a different perspective.

- In the first position you'll be you looking out through your own eyes.
- In the second you'll be the other party, be it one person or a group it works the same.)
- In the third position you get to step back and have a look at the two parties more dispassionately.

1. Go to the first position. Ask: what are my preferred outcomes and my fallback position?
2. Go to the second position. Ask: what are their preferred outcomes and their fallback position?

3. Go to the third position. Given what you've just said in both the first and second positions, what strikes you about the two parties? What needs to happen so that they can have a productive meeting? Consider what might be the next step.

4. Given what you now know, review the range of possibilities open to you – and to them.

Having the confidence to say 'no'

There is an old business adage: never do a deal that you couldn't afford to walk away from!

Too often people fear they will lose out if they don't accept the terms on offer. But being able to say 'no' is just as important as being able to say 'yes', and it requires a certain kind of confidence: however attractive whatever seems to be on offer, ultimately you need to be able to go with your own instincts and not be seduced.

My client Greg was a success: his new business, to everyone's surprise, was flourishing, his job was fulfilling and all should have been well in his world – only Greg was starting to notice that as the business became more and more successful, his business partner Julie became more and more volatile.

Stressed by the unexpected and rapid success of the business, Julie was starting to act strangely. She took to calling Greg at all hours, checking up on him, and before long Greg began to feel hounded. The business was working, but the partnership wasn't. After six months of this, Greg had begun to feel the price he was paying – Julie's instability and unpredictability – was too high.

'Julie changed,' Greg told me. Certainly he was seeing another side of her, but she was still the same person. Now, though, she was dealing with what for her was the stress of success.

After a lot of soul-searching – the business was going from strength to strength, after all – Greg made a confident decision.

He decided to walk away and start anew. It was a bold move. That was ten years ago and he's never looked back. I know this because when he decided that it was time to bring others into his new venture, he called me and we made sure that this time his partners would be people who, among other things, could cope with success!

Chapter 7

Confidence, Health and Wealth

Health Confidence: Taking Charge of Your Own Health

Health and wealth are two areas in which what you believe can have a big impact on what is possible for you. To show you what I mean, let me tell you about a client of mine who had recently been diagnosed as having Type II diabetes. He wanted to do something about this. He was surprised to learn that changing his diet and increasing his level of exercise might well produce substantial change. Six months later, he returned to his physician to repeat the tests, confident that they would show an improvement. Sure enough they did. The results now came back negative. He was over the moon and felt pretty pleased with himself for having been able to turn things around. However, the nurse regarded these results with some suspicion and decided to do the tests again – with the same result. Unable to credit that such a change could occur, she said the original results six months previously must have been erroneous. Because she could not believe that such a change was possible, she needed to explain the result by adjusting (the previous) reality. Thus she could avoid any challenge to her beliefs.

People often say, 'I'll believe it when I see it.' But in truth it's often the case that you'll only see it when you believe it – or more accurately, you'll only see what's in front of your eyes when you believe that it is possible.

So what do you believe about your health? Try jotting down your beliefs. For most people this is quite a challenge, as they've never really thought about it. So to get you started, let me tell you some of my own beliefs which I've become aware of over the years:

1. I can make my health better or worse.
2. What I do – and don't do – now will affect my health in times to come. If I want to be healthy, I need to make the investment in myself that good health requires.
3. No health tradition has all the answers. The more approaches I'm familiar with, the more chances I have of finding what will work best for me and others.
4. Health is a matter of degree. At any moment each of us is on a health continuum. At one end lies radiant well-being and boundless vitality, at the other end chronic ill-health leading to death.
5. No condition is untreatable. We just may not know what to do for the best – so let's begin finding out by trial and error.

Please understand that when I tell you these are some of my beliefs, I'm not claiming that these statements are actually true. Technically, each is really a presupposition I choose to make. Beliefs are how we make sense of the world. But for most of us, whether or not they are true, beliefs shape our world because we act as if they were true.

I find these five beliefs are all really useful in helping me shape my own destiny and, when shared, they offer my clients' the maximum range of health-promoting possibilities. Take belief number five. If you believe that no condition is untreatable, you'll be interested in any evidence that a particular treatment regimen may help, be it from unexpected quarters or happening in ways we don't yet understand. Here's one current example: we now have extremely good data to demonstrate that when people with Parkinson's disease begin dancing, many of their symptoms spontaneously and immediately cease for the duration of their dancing. Right now hypotheses are still being generated about why this should be the case, but we don't really know what's going on.

I was struck by the mindset of one of the physicians working with those Parkinson's patients. Commenting on the findings in an NBC interview, Dr Abraham Lieberman simply said, 'I don't know how my iPhone works, but it works.' That's a very different mindset from the nurse who needed to rewrite my client's medical history so that her beliefs would not be challenged. It's also a classic NLP way of thinking: if it works, let's use it.

EXERCISE: Your Health Beliefs

What do you believe about your health generally? Mull this over for a few days, then fill in five beliefs below. (You could start by seeing if you agree with my beliefs, above.) Then ask yourself: do these beliefs serve you or do you need to change them? If you need to change, one place to begin will be the ABC approach (see page 78). Also look for counter-examples that make clear other alternatives are possible.

1. . . . .
2. . . . .
3. . . . .
4. . . . .
5. . . . .

The importance of feedback

Being able to track how we are doing is fundamental to feeling confident we know what's going on. To know what's going on you have to pay attention to the feedback that you're getting, whether it's external (your annual review; your partner's reaction to a suggestion of yours) or internal (this activity makes me feel good; this food makes me feel sick). To experience health – and wealth – confidence you need to have some good feedback to let you know how you're doing.

Some feedback is instant: touch a hot plate and you immediately recoil. Quite often, though, we experience what is known as delayed feedback. Some years ago my dental check-up revealed some inflammation in a part of my gum. I was told what to do and I went away and did it. Six months later I went back – and it was still the same. Obviously there was something I wasn't doing right. I needed to shorten the feedback loop so that I could correct my behaviour much more quickly. For three months I saw the dental hygienist once a month. She was then able to make suggestions and as a result, relatively quickly, the issue was completely resolved. The tighter the feedback loop, the more useful the feedback.

Feedback can boost your confidence in at least three different ways:

- **Feedback is a motivator.** One of my clients came to realise that drinking alcohol exacerbated the chronic pain he'd been experiencing from a car accident five years previously. Suddenly he was powerfully motivated to stop drinking – and he began to experience less pain than he had known at any time for those five years.
- **Feedback is empowering.** This was the first time he had any indication that he could actually affect his level of pain. Now he no longer felt he was on the receiving end of something over which he had no control.

- **Feedback can change beliefs.** Until then, he had not believed that the pain could be under his control at all. And he certainly didn't believe his alcohol consumption affected his pain. I suggested to him that if he drank more than usual, he would feel more pain. Eager to disprove my prediction, he did so – but found I was right. That's how he first came to understand that he could influence his pain.

Learning to pay attention to feedback

Health feedback comes in many forms, not just medical tests. Most of the time it's not that there isn't any feedback; it's more a question of:

- Do we recognise what is happening as feedback?
- Do we pay attention to it?
- Do we give it credence?
- Do we act on it?

Take somatic responses. Many people just don't pay much attention to them. Even when they do they often don't know what to make of them. Yawning is a great example. I was in a meeting recently with one of my staff, who's very committed and has loads of energy. It's about 12.30 p.m. and I notice she's stifling a yawn, and another, and another. She's not bored and she's not tired. So I tell her that yawning often correlates with a drop in blood sugar and is a signal to eat. She didn't know this. Since that time she's learnt to eat when this happens, with immediate benefits.

Our somatic responses are often invaluable forms of feedback and can even have predictive power. I know, for instance, that if I begin to get a kind of ache in my left ear, I need to get more rest and ease off. If I don't, I'm much more likely to be susceptible to infection – which, of course, if it takes hold, will force me to take more rest and ease off.

Many times my work has involved encouraging people not only to pay attention to such feedback but to take it seriously and then act on it. Why does this matter? *Because feedback is communication from you to yourself.* In learning to pay attention to this internal feedback, you are learning to listen to the wisdom within.

What feedback mechanisms do you have in place that enable you to know how you're doing with your health? Here are some important points to remember:

- **You need to know what strengthens you and what weakens you.** This varies from person to person. One client realised that as long as he got good sound sleep, he could handle pretty much anything else. Another said that feeling connected to her adult children is incredibly health-giving for her. When you know what gives you the maximum return, you can make it a real priority.
- **You need some basic information, so be curious.** Did you know, for instance, that an increasing number of studies are suggesting dental health may be a predictor of illnesses that affect other areas of the body? These range from heart disease to dementia.[6] 'That means ensuring good dental health is a good preventative health measure for your whole body.
- **If you're not certain, have the courage to ask.** Too many people have unanswered questions about their health. Go and ask someone who's professionally qualified. When you see health professionals, it's fine to ask follow-up questions once you've had time to get clear what you're not clear about.

EXERCISE: Your Health Feedback Loops

Here are some questions to get you paying attention to your own feedback:

Internal feedback

- What makes you feel really good? How does this register in your body?
- What are your telltale symptoms that you're overdoing it?
- What is particularly good for you – and makes you feel great?
- What is particularly undermining for your health?
- What are your weak spots physically? How do you take care of them?

External feedback

- Do you have regular dental check-ups?
- Do you have any kind of medical check-up periodically?

The power of structure

Each year, with the start of a new year, millions of people around the world make resolutions to exercise more, lose weight or drink less. These are the classic New Year's resolutions. But as American comedian Joey Adams once said, 'May all your troubles last as long as your New Year's resolutions!'

Most people find that although they are quite genuine in wanting to make a change, their New Year's resolutions don't last. This doesn't have much to do with the resolutions. It has everything to do with whether you have supporting structures in place to sustain you over time.

Here's the thing: in the moment that we commit to do something and make that resolution, we genuinely have a feeling that that's what we want to do. But feelings are transient and forever changing. As long as you feel the way you did when you made that resolution, you stand a chance of making that change. But actually, in any given day, you experience a whole variety of internal states, only some of which are likely to be supportive of that New Year's resolution.

If you want to ensure your success in making any changes that support your health, you'll need to create structures that can support you when your internal state may not. The structures that work invariably ensure that any new behaviour or regime can be *regular, consistent* and *ongoing*.

Routines would be an obvious example of such a supportive structure. Involving others in your routines is often essential for success. In my case, I know that while I want the benefits of having worked out, that doesn't mean I will necessarily do it! So, ten years ago, I decided to delegate motivation – ever since I've had a trainer who turns up twice a week, whether I feel like working out or not.

EXERCISE: Putting Your Structures in Place

So what structures do *you* need to have in place? If you don't have them, you're stacking the cards against success. Either you're not in the mood at the right time, or sometimes people can just feel overwhelmed by what needs to be done.

Ask yourself:

1. What needs to happen so that the changes needed can be broken down into manageable chunks?
2. What might those manageable chunks be?
3. What is the best sequence of steps for me?
4. What structures would need to be in place to ensure my consistent success?
5. So what do I need to do?

Health challenge: burnout

The splendidly named Herbert J. Freudenberger was the man who first coined the term burnout in 1974. He had a reputation for working very long hours, but he did not experience burnout. And that's important, because burnout is not about working hard or being fatigued.

For a time, Freudenberger was working in a free clinic for drug addicts in Haight-Ashbury which was staffed by volunteers. The work was really tough and he noticed that, when discouraged, those volunteers would often try even harder – only to feel ineffectual. Some said they had started with high hopes of making a difference but felt they were achieving less and less as time went on.

What he identified was a toxic combination of exhaustion, disillusionment and feeling ineffectual. This is what lies at the heart of burnout.

In NLP we have done a lot of work on what are known as thresholds. Some thresholds are positive – your confidence builds, at a certain point you are emboldened to take a risk and you've never looked back since. Other thresholds are negative. When you hear someone say, 'I just snapped!' they're probably telling you how they went over a threshold.

Understanding burnout as a threshold can be really useful. Understanding how you go over a threshold and how to get back means you can really make a difference to what's going on.

When I ask people to think of the different things they're called upon to do, it's usually the case that we can divide them into three categories: those they enjoy, those they really don't enjoy and those that are pretty ho hum. Those they enjoy tend to nourish and energise them, while those they don't enjoy tend to drain and deplete them.

Take any given day, week or month and simply by reviewing what you did and which of these three categories it falls under, you can rapidly determine the current state of play. I often find it useful to ask clients to write this down in columns under the three headings – draining, neutral and nourishing – so they can clearly see the current balance. You might want to get a piece of paper and do this too.

Imagine if 75 per cent of what you do at work shows up somewhere to the left of neutral. That might look like a recipe for burnout if it continues over time. But suppose at the same time that 75 per cent of what goes on in your primary relationship is to the right of neutral and so very nourishing. You might well be able to tolerate work because of what happens outside of it. So a balance of different interests could be good for your health and enable you to cope. However, it doesn't do anything to address what's wrong at work.

But what if you've invested your all in that one particular domain? Now there is no refuge. If 75 per cent of work is draining, you're going to experience it acutely. And you'll probably be much more susceptible to going over the threshold and experiencing burnout.

Whenever burnout happens, people will probably reveal some of the following symptoms. They're likely to feel physically depleted and lacking in energy; emotionally exhausted, frustrated and volatile; more susceptible to infection because of lowered immunity; less invested in personal relationships because they feel they just don't have anything left over to give; and increasingly pessimistic because they don't see any way they can improve things.

Too often people I've worked with who are experiencing burnout have got used to a second-rate experience of being alive. Some of them have tried to escape their present hell by making external changes: they've quit their job or a relationship. Some have emigrated. Such actions can be powerfully liberating. However, if people don't make some internal changes, there is a real danger that the same problems will show up again. And this can affect both your overall sense of well-being and also your physical health.

Now for the good news: burnout is reversible

In a way, burnout is simply feedback from you to yourself. It's telling you that things are out of balance, that there is not enough in some part – perhaps many parts – of your life that is satisfying, nourishing and meaningful for you. You can change this. And you can start today.

EXERCISE: Balance – the Antidote to Burnout

Step 1: Take stock of what you do and how it affects your energy levels

Note whether each activity is draining, neutral or nourishing. Ideally, you'll replace draining activities with nourishing ones. If that's not always possible, consider how you can minimise their impact on you – perhaps by doing them less or differently or with others.

Step 2: Get more balance in your life

Say you've been heavily invested in work. What do you need to do to nourish your social, emotional and spiritual life – and how about tending to your health and fitness needs? By investing more energy in areas of your life that may have been neglected, you revitalise and rebalance yourself.

Step 3: Introduce change incrementally

Too often people want the comic-book version of change – with one bound he was free! In fact, if you start making small changes in the direction of more energising and nourishing activity and keep doing this, you will gradually produce a huge change in how you experience being alive.

Creating a Compelling Future

First, make sure you have a future!

Many years ago, I was asked to work with some guys who were HIV+. At that time, HIV was pretty much seen as a death sentence. What struck me was that you could divide these patients into two groups: those who were planning for a future and those who seemed to have no sense of any future. With the latter, it was as if they'd already shut it down. With them, my response was to ask questions which would shock them into a new awareness that their future was not over – the future did exist.

I made a note of one of these exchanges at the time:

Ian: So, will you be dead by teatime?
Patient: No!
Ian: Going to be around for breakfast tomorrow?
Patient: Of course.
Ian: How about the day after?
Patient: Yes, of course.
Ian: Think you'll make it through to this time next week?
Patient: I'm sure I will.

In this way, we began to reclaim this patient's immediate future as something real which he could know was going to happen. Of course, a week can become a month, a month a year and so on. Whenever I worked this way, something remarkable would happen. As soon as there was some kind of imaginable future, the person would begin to feel more alive and begin to engage more. They would also become more open to planning something for that future. This could start with something as simple as fixing a day next week to go to the movies. But it would soon move into what it was they wanted to do with whatever time they did have left.

When people feel they have no future, they lose hope. The converse is also true: when people lose hope, they lose their future.

When a person loses hope, they no longer believe a health goal is attainable. I had a client who, when we met, had been in constant pain for five years. She'd got to the point of believing that nothing was really going to make a change. So when in the course of our session she had the experience of a complete cessation of the pain, at first she couldn't believe what was happening, and then she said a very interesting thing: 'I dare not believe this could go on – I couldn't stand the disappointment of it stopping.' So even as she was experiencing what she wanted, she was fearing the loss of it. It was useful therefore to create repeated experiences for her of what was possible so that she could dare to believe again in a different – pain-free – future. In this way we made it safe for her to have hope for the future.

Second, make sure your future is a good one

In his book *Spontaneous Healing*, the American doctor Andrew Weil tells of a Finnish patient, still mobile, who, after numerous tests, had a meeting with the head neurologist. He told her she had MS. Then he stepped out of his office and returned with a wheelchair which he told her to sit in. She protested and questioned why she should sit in the wheelchair. His reply? He wanted her to buy one and sit in it for an hour a day to practise for when she would be totally disabled! That neurologist was trying to prepare his patient for a future he saw as inevitable. She, however, didn't find this very helpful.

By definition, the future has not yet arrived. In matters of health this can work for us and against us. For us, because there's time to prepare and make any necessary changes; against us, because we can kid ourselves that though we're doing something that's not good for us, there doesn't seem to be any immediate ill effect, so why worry?

Some years ago, an interesting television series called *Turn Back Your Body Clock* was broadcast in the UK. Dr Una Coales would give a variety of people a graphic demonstration of how their organs would look on the inside if they kept eating, drinking or smoking in the way they were presently doing. Without exception, these graphic representations of what the participants were doing to themselves had a profound impact. Often people would be moved to tears and say things like: 'I just didn't realise.' Was this literally true? Maybe; maybe not. But what made the difference was that the graphics suddenly made it very clear that present actions will have future consequences. In this way, Dr Coales created a compelling future which her patients wanted to move away from. Would this be useful for you – or your doctor – to do for you?

Either way, it's also going to be really useful if you can create a compelling future that you want to move towards. Something that is attractive has attractor properties, that is to say it pulls you towards it. That's what you want your future healthy state – your future healthy version of you – to do: to attract you towards it so that you naturally begin to modify your health.

EXERCISE: Create Your Compelling Future

This exercise uses sub-modalities to make your future extraordinarily attractive.

1. Create a visual representation of a future you: healthy and vibrant.
2. Make it into a movie and make that movie big, bright and colourful, in clear focus and with sound.
3. Then step into the movie and feel how it is to be this way.
4. Now play this movie in front of you up to your right. (If you're left-handed and having it to the right doesn't feel comfortable

for you, try up to your left.) Experiment with the position and distance to find where it feels most compelling and attractive. (You may even feel that it's pulling you towards it.) Then lock it in.

5. Run this movie at least once a week. One client I know runs their movie before they go to sleep each night. Let it evolve and just get better over time.

Your Health Is Your Wealth

Over the past twenty years, I have been involved in numerous international training initiatives with colleagues around the world. I've been lucky because they have pretty much all been successful, but it's striking that the ones which took the most work to promote have always been health programmes. I think the reason for this is that too many people only become interested in their health when something's gone wrong.

It is no secret that eating vast quantities of junk food, never exercising and smoking is an excellent way to speed up the life cycle of human beings so they reach the end faster! I want you to be confident in your health and your body's ability to heal: it's amazing how your body takes care of business without you really knowing what's going on. But you shouldn't get complacent and think there's nothing that you need to do. The health-building exercises in this chapter will give you a lot of benefits. One final piece of advice; please remember the wise words of a Chinese herbalist I know: 'The best thing anyone can do to improve their health is to increase their happiness.'

* * * * *

It's fitting we should focus on both health and wealth in the same chapter as there is an amazing amount of overlap between the two. All but one of the exercises we have just done for health can be used just as effectively with regard to wealth. So, in a sense, much of the ground is already mapped out and ready for us to explore. However, as anyone who has had the experience of a loss of health – and the loss of well-being that goes with it – can tell you, in a very real sense your health *is* your wealth.

Self-worth trumps net worth

What's really important about wealth is that it has very little to do with how much money you have in the bank and everything to do with how wealthy you feel – which means, of course, that it is entirely subjective. You may – and I've had quite a few clients like this – have millions in the bank and still not feel wealthy. Because what wealth really boils down to is you and your idea of how much is enough. Your wealth is entirely relative and depends on your aspirations and what you need to realise them.

Starting in late 2008, collective confidence in the banking system plummeted as people watched their assets disappearing, leaving them feeling angry and helpless. True confidence is the ability to feel good about yourself, irrespective of the level of income you may or may not have. It does not matter how great your financial net worth is; it will never be enough unless your sense of self-worth is sufficient. In other words, self-worth trumps net worth, every time.

If you have a robust sense of self then you can and will handle life's ups and downs, including financial challenges, more confidently. While having more money may raise your confidence levels temporarily, this is a false buzz because acquiring more money can never make you more *sustainably* confident. In fact, if you are using money to try and boost your confidence, you are engaged in high-risk behaviour. Money can always be taken away, which, if you have made it the one thing that gives you your sense of worth, will leave you feeling very vulnerable. As Frank Wheeler says about his own life circumstances in the book *Revolutionary Road*: 'Knowing what you've got, knowing what you need, knowing what you can do without – that's inventory control.'

As with health, taking the long view is what's going to deliver the best return. Developing your financial IQ is going to empower you and this will make you more confident. Otherwise, even if you win the lottery you don't necessarily get to feel any more confident. Being wealthy doesn't mean you can't still make a real mess of things. Michael Jackson is a tragic example. Here was a millionaire living the lifestyle of a billionaire. Result? Endless financial hassles. So let's have a look at what you can do that's going to strengthen your confidence and build your wealth.

EXERCISE: **Your Wealth Beliefs**

As with your health, these are going to have a significant impact on how you behave and what you believe is even possible. So what are yours? Here are some of mine to get you started. You may agree or you may not, but these will give you something to bounce off.

1. What I do – and don't do – now will affect my wealth in times to come. If I want future wealth, I need to make the investment now that this requires.
2. A healthy cash flow is critical to a sense of well-being – more so even than capital accumulation.
3. No one advisor has all the answers.
4. Wealth is a matter of degree. Only I can decide what it means to me.

5. I can always address what's going on and improve it if I choose to be informed and proactive.

What do you believe about wealth generally? Mull it over for a few days, then fill in five beliefs below. Then ask yourself: do these beliefs serve you or do you need to change them? If you need to change, one place to begin will be the ABC approach (see page 78). Also look for counter-examples that make clear other alternatives are possible.

1. . . . .

2. . . . .

3. . . . .

4. . . . .

5. . . . .

Paying attention to feedback

You need to find out where you stand financially so you can then take action. Not knowing only increases anxiety. Over half the people I meet worry about their finances and their financial future but are not sure what to do. Basic financial planning is empowering. If it's useful, get someone skilled to help you pri-oritise your financial goals – what you don't know *can* hurt you!

You need some basic information

Determine your net monthly and annual income. Then add up your debts, including balances on car loans and credit cards.

Where's the money going?

List your major monthly expenses: for example, mortgage, car payments, credit cards, insurance, food, travel, utilities.

If you're not certain, have the courage to ask

Call creditors to get the current state of play. Seek expert input if it's going to help you be in charge.

EXERCISE: Your Wealth Feedback Loops

Here are some questions to get you paying attention to your own feedback:

Internal feedback

- Are you paying attention to and tracking how you feel emotionally about the current state of your financial affairs?
- What are doing with this emotional information?
- What are your weak spots? How will you take care of them?
- What can you do financially that's going to make you feel good?

Internal feedback

- Are you paying attention to and tracking financial information – i.e. feedback – that comes in the form of bank statements, invoices etc?

The power of structure

If you want to ensure your success in making any changes that support your wealth, you'll need to create structures that can support you. The structures that work invariably ensure that any new behaviour or regime can be *regular, consistent* and *ongoing*. These need to apply to what you earn, what you save and what you spend.

Routines would be an obvious example of such a supportive structure. If, for instance, you curb your expenditure so that it is appropriate to income and you save on a regular basis, and if that saving actually happens *before* you start spending, you *will* accumulate over time. Never underestimate the power of incremental saving. If you want to explore this idea further, read *The Millionaire Next Door* by Thomas Stanley and William Danko.

So what structures do *you* need to have in place to do this? If you don't have these to support you, you're stacking the cards against success.

EXERCISE: Putting Your Structures in Place

Ask yourself the following questions:

1. What needs to happen so that the changes needed can be broken down into bite-size chunks?
2. What bite-size chunks would I find manageable?
3. What is the best sequence of steps for me?
4. What structures would need to be in place to ensure my consistent success?
5. So what do I need to do?

If you want to create a more compelling – and wealthy! – future, you'll want to repeat the Create Your Compelling Future exercise from page 154. This time visualise a future you who is healthy *and* wealthy.

For good health and great wealth – celebrate!

Lots of people don't even recognise, let alone celebrate, their own triumphs, but they should, because making time and finding a way to do so is one of the best confidence-building exercises I know of.

I often describe this to clients as a punctuation exercise, like stopping what you are doing to press the refresh button on the story of your life so far. How often do you stop to celebrate where you are right now, how you got here and all those personal triumphs along the way? Do you have a space in your life where this can happen, or are you so busy rushing from one thing to the next that by the time you come up for breath another year will have flown by?

Celebrating the good times calls our attention to what is working in our lives, and knowing what works is a fast-track route to boosting and maintaining confidence from one chapter of our lives to the next. Working out what is significant to you – what matters enough for you to celebrate it – also helps you to focus on what matters and why.

Here are some questions to get you going:

- What – today, right now – can you celebrate about you?
- What *new* things have you done over the last year?
- What *outstanding* things have you done over the last year?
- What have you done over the last year that you can celebrate today?

If you want to get a more rounded perspective ask your friends. Tell them you're updating your Confidence Resumé! Your friends will highlight your unique gifts and abilities for you because they see them more clearly than you do. It might make you squirm to ask, but you will find their responses very confidence-inspiring and you'll end up feeling you have plenty to celebrate!

PART III

LIVING WITH CONFIDENCE

Chapter 8

What to Do When Confidence Deserts You

I t's easy to feel confident when everything is going your way. But if you want to live confidently, you'll need to know how to handle yourself when your confidence is threatened.

Such threats can come in various forms, but one that people often don't think about is simply the passage of time. Anyone who wants to live with confidence needs to consider: how can I move through the different stages of my life feeling equally confident in myself? In theory, you can be any kind of forty-, fifty- or sixty-year-old you choose. But I have worked with quite a few clients who have experienced a loss of confidence as they have grown older because they felt they were being relegated to the sidelines. Even if you're confident in yourself, external changes can make you do a double take. I had a very successful client who in the run-up to his sixtieth birthday started getting mail about his state pension and winter fuel allowance: he said indignantly, 'The last thing I need is a bloody bus pass!'

Whatever the particular circumstances, an ounce of prevention is worth a pound of cure, so I want you to be able to recognise quickly the signs of a loss of confidence. Then we can look at strategies that enable a person to do something about it.

Loss of Confidence – Earthquake or Erosion?

There are two key ways in which we can lose confidence. The first, and most obvious, is what I call the *earthquake*. A shock, a big change and usually something we feel we have had no control over produces a sudden loss of confidence that triggers feelings of disorientation and loss. Because it involves loss, it is often experienced as bereavement. This can be triggered, for instance, by the loss of a job (you're let go from work), the loss of a role (the children leave home and mother now has an empty nest), the loss of a relationship (your partner has an affair or walks out). This means it can be very painful not only for the person going through it, but also the people who care about them who feel powerless to help.

The other, more insidious way that we can lose confidence is through a slow attrition – what I call *erosion*. Just as a leaky tap, if left unfixed, can fill, overflow and flood, so can a long, slow loss of confidence. When this happens, you may know dimly at first that something in your life isn't as great as it was. Then you become aware that it still hasn't gotten better. Then you realise it's deteriorating, but only quite slowly. It could be anything – your job prospects, your business, your health, your relationship – but you have no idea what to do about it. Gradually you become resigned and your confidence deteriorates further.

I have yet to meet a person who hasn't experienced one of these at some time in their life. Whether it's earthquake or erosion, a loss of confidence has some telltale signs. Typically:

- You are no longer confident you can make things happen.
- You are no longer confident you can think things through.
- You are no longer confident you can change your circumstances.
- You no longer have confidence in your future.
- You no longer feel confident in yourself.
- You no longer feel confident about who you can trust and rely on.

At its most extreme, a severe loss of confidence will result in a person becoming withdrawn, even hermit-like. Not surprisingly, depression can then kick in.

In such a state it's hard to hold on to any sense of direction (*I know where I am going*) or hope (*I believe many things are possible*). There is a loss of purpose and that optimistic sense of possibility. Sometimes people stop valuing themselves and launch into endless punitive internal dialogues. Not surprisingly, they can lose any joy in living as a result. If you've had even a taste of this at some time in your life, you'll know that it can be pretty bleak. But, as I have said to clients in this position, however bleak you are feeling, remember this: you may not be able to change what happened to shatter your confidence, but you can *always* do something about how you are dealing with it.

EXERCISE: Converting Breakdowns into Breakthroughs

This is something you can do to review any time in your life and get a different perspective on it. For many people, it's an easy and surprisingly effective way of learning from your experience and realising where you are now.

Think of a specific time when you faced some kind of adversity and rose to the challenge. Somehow you came through. It could be anything from family crisis to a business bust-up. Write a letter to someone you trust and care about and tell them honestly what happened, how it made you feel and how you feel about it now. You are not going to post this letter – ever. You are simply taking stock in retrospect, putting your feelings and thoughts down on paper and telling someone you trust because then you can be honest.

Before you draft your letter, ask yourself the following questions:

- What was your role in the crisis or bust-up?
- What impact did the kind of people you were hanging out with have on how you handled things?
- How did they affect your confidence before and after the crisis?
- What kind of people are you hanging out with now?
- How do they affect your confidence?
- You survived this crisis or bust-up. How does knowing that you survived make you feel?
- How does knowing this affect your confidence as you go forward?

When you have written your letter, read it aloud to yourself and notice the confidence journey you have taken since the start of the crisis and its resolution through to today. As you look back, what would you say worked to help boost your confidence?

Sometimes it's only when the old routines break down that it is possible for you to break through. Now I want to show you how.

Confidence challenge 1: uncertainty

For many people, the economic crisis that began in 2008 gave rise to some very tough times. Some lost their jobs, some even their homes. Relationships were put under strain and some went past the point of no return. And a lot of people lost a lot of sleep.

However, it's also true to say that the majority of people still had a job, still had a home and still had a relationship. So you could say: what was all the fuss about? However, I think you'd only say this if you were from another planet! The problem was that people experienced massively increased levels of uncertainty. One of the things we know about human beings is that we find it more stressful not knowing how things may turn out, than knowing they will turn out badly.

Some years ago, the Interstate 35W Bridge collapsed in Minneapolis. Dorothy Svendson was one of many relatives left not knowing what had happened to her son, a construction worker on the bridge. As she said: 'It's the not knowing that eats you up.' The same is true even when it's not a life and death situation. As one client said to me, 'one of the hardest things about living with IBS [irritable bowel syndrome] is the not knowing what triggers the flare-ups'.

As Harvard Psychology professor Daniel Gilbert pointed out in an interesting blog, recent research underlines just how debilitating and anxiety-provoking uncertainty can be. In an experiment at Maastricht University subjects were given twenty electric shocks. Some knew that they would receive twenty intense shocks; others knew there would be seventeen mild shocks and only three intense shocks, but not the order in which they would come. Guess who handled this situation better? Those who knew they were going to get twenty intense shocks prepared themselves and adjusted for what was to come. The other group found it much harder. Judging by standard fear indicators such as sweating and heart rate, it was this second group that registered much higher fear levels. So although they experienced less physical discomfort, they actually worried more.[7]

Nor is this an isolated study. To take just one other example, researchers at the University of British Columbia looked at people at risk of developing Huntington's Disease. A year after testing, those who had been informed that they had a high likelihood of developing the condition were still happier than those who had not been informed of their risk level but had been left hanging.

So how does all this apply in a practical way to our overall confidence? Well, let me put it this way. How would you feel if, like one of my clients, you didn't know if you'd keep your job, be able to pay the mortgage, whether your partner was having an affair or if the stress you were feeling might be compromising your health in the long-term? Some people can tolerate quite high levels of uncertainty; others have a much lower threshold. Either way, it's important to recognise that uncertainty can be a potent stress factor and that such stress can impact on both your confidence and, over time, even on your health.

Recently, I was coaching a couple who were having a tough time of it. We met for one hour. At the beginning they were both tense and she often close to tears. She was upset because her daughter was getting engaged in the summer and she wanted the family to be able to celebrate with a proper party. But then there was their son's upcoming twenty-first birthday too. The wife was afraid that if she asked for the two parties she had set her heart on, her husband would hit the roof about the cost. His car-hire business was already suffering in the recession; he had no idea what they were budgeting for and so felt anxious about being able to fund it.

This couple – and their relationship – were experiencing a high level of stress born of uncertainty and a lack of clarity. The effect was to put them at odds with each other. By the end of the session, we had arrived at a manageable budget for the celebrations the wife had hoped they could offer their children; she was smiling, he was relieved because he knew he could finance both parties and they were hugging each other. Removing the uncertainty removed the stress and the alienation. Now they shared a common goal and had come together again. Uncertainty had created fear and anxiety, strong emotions which can mask – even erode – love. By the end of our coaching session, this couple could once again feel the tenderness and the love they have for each other.

EXERCISE: Getting to Grips with Uncertainty

How much uncertainty are you – and those you care about – living with right now?

Get a pen and paper and write down the answers to the following questions:

1. How long has this uncertainty been going on?
2. How long can you tolerate this uncertainty?
3. Is there any end in sight?
4. What makes you feel stable and grounded?
5. What do you need to do to ensure you have more of this in your life now?
6. Who can help you achieve this?
7. So what's the next step?

Confidence challenge 2: worry and anxiety

Most people have had the experience of living through turbulent times. However, at such times a lot of the turbulence people experience is on the inside and it manifests as worry and anxiety.

Worry is what you think about – often in the wee small hours, over and over. Anxiety is the physical feelings and emotions you experience. Both can be very useful if they make you look hard at what's happening, encourage you to prepare for the future and explore new avenues, and motivate you to take action. So both have their place – but both can get out of control.

When you're worrying, you often create a narrative: it's the story we tell ourselves that generates the feelings. Sometimes that story is realistic. Often, though, it is not – hence Mark Twain's observation: 'I have known a great many troubles, but most of them never happened.'

Worrying tends to have a pattern – both in how it starts and what it's about – and it's worth knowing what your pattern is. Ask yourself:

- What triggers worry in you?
- What are the stories you keep rerunning?
- What are the recurrent themes?
- What changes your state so you stop worrying?

Anxiety is an intensely kinaesthetic experience and people experience it differently. I'm always interested to know how my clients do anxiety. While one may somatise it all in the stomach, another may experience it more as racing heart and sweaty palms. As a practitioner, when you know the individual style it becomes much easier to recommend appropriate counter-measures. While, for instance, both walking and massage can be extraordinarily therapeutic antidotes, one may suit a person much better.

People can habituate to a high level of distress. That's why there's always a danger that both worry and anxiety can move from being acute to chronic.

I find it very useful to have clients self-assess on three key parameters. The drivers I pay particular attention to are intensity, frequency and duration. Here's what you can do:

- Measure the level of intensity on a scale of 1 to 10.
- With frequency, review how often you're having the experience: hourly, daily, weekly and monthly?
- With duration, consider how long the experience lasts – minutes, hours or days?

The greater the intensity, frequency and duration, the more beneficial it will be to learn new ways of breaking out of what can so easily become an habitual state. This is particularly worth doing because if not addressed, worry and anxiety that goes on and on can sometimes be the precursor to depression – which is just about the opposite of confidence.

However, sometimes events may overwhelm us and when that happens we may not feel able to be bigger than the fears we are confronting. At these times, two additional strategies will be useful. First, look for where you can experience some degree of control or influence, no matter how trivial it may seem. Exercise that control and you'll reduce any feelings of helplessness and powerlessness.

Second, ask yourself whether you are willing to experiment with letting go and knowing that you don't know. Sometimes this can be the most freeing path of all.

Given that we cannot control the world, we might as well learn how to control our fears. Being able to realistically assess a threat, take steps to address it and then change your internal state so that you can once more be master of your fate is an extraordinarily empowering thing to do. It does wonders for your confidence!

7 Steps to Address Worry and Anxiety

1. Do a reality check. Ask yourself, is my worry realistic? How clear am I about what I fear? Develop a plan of action.
2. Think again! If your thoughts are taking you in a repetitive or downward spiral, think some different thoughts – literally. Many of our thoughts are just habits. Maybe it's time to acquire new habits of thinking. Learn to have some different thoughts about what you're worrying about – try

using your ABC model again (see page 78). Also sometimes it can be useful just to switch your attention and engage with different aspects of the world.

3. Stop obsessing! Thought stopping is actually a very effective technique. Internally – or out loud – you simply say in a loud firm voice: 'Stop!' Try it – you'll be surprised at its effectiveness.

4. Quite deliberately breathe fully and freely to counteract fearful tendencies which invariably constrict breathing.

5. Engage in physical exercise that can burn off excess adrenalin and return you to a calmer state. Running or brisk walking will do it – but what about dancing? Make the activity fun and enjoyable.

6. Focus on others and their needs so that you don't get so wrapped up in yourself. Being generous with your time is truly low-cost and can be a great antidote to anxiety.

7. Work out what counts as safe and solid ground for you and what gives you comfort. Determine how you can have some of this everyday.

Regaining Confidence after an Accident

Accidents can have a big impact on our confidence. My friend Harriet tripped while carrying a tray of glasses, severing an artery in her right hand. Lying in the back of the ambulance hooked up to an oxygen mask and terrified by the amount of blood pumping out of the gaping wound, she could not believe what had happened. The paramedic started talking to her, telling her that he had served in the army, where colleagues who had suffered similar wounds – 'bleeders, we called them' –

had permanently lost the use of the hand. Being right-handed, Harriet duly imagined the worst, especially when, as they reached the hospital, the paramedic began shouting: 'We've got a bleeder!' (Notice how this is an Identity level statement. Because this is a very charged time, the power of these words is likely to be even greater than usual – as Harriet found out later.)

The cut was so deep that Harriet had to keep her hand bandaged for two months. Since she could not drive, wash-up, work or even write a shopping list, she had plenty of time to bear witness to her shattering loss of confidence. At first she couldn't bear to look at glass in any shape or form. She drank from plastic cups and would avoid touching anything that she could imagine might shatter in her hand. Every day for the first two weeks she had to have her wound checked and dressed. It was three weeks before she could bring herself to look at the jagged gash on her hand. And that's when we began working together – hands free – over the phone.

There are some wonderful NLP processes designed to promote trauma resolution. Some were specifically developed to promote physical healing as well. (If this is something you'd like to explore, see Resources for details of finding a trained practitioner.) All of them involve getting some real separation between you and the traumatic episode. Learning how to run a movie of the episode so she could see herself having the experience while remaining outside it and no longer feeling overwhelmed or having the bad feelings associated with it was the first step. (N.B. Harriet was not denying what had happened, but she was able to remember the event in a way which didn't bother her like before.) The second step was to recode the trauma so that she could create a new ending for the event. In this version, she was not actually hurt at all because she acted differently so that it didn't happen. Doing this allowed her to create a new muscle memory of what could have been, as well as ensuring she would be well prepared and act differently if there were ever similar circumstances in the future. Doing this frequently seems to help the physical healing process; I think this is because it unlocks whatever the body is holding onto following a trauma, rather like a muscle can be held tight and then released through massage. As a result, it's not uncommon for people to report feeling less pain or other physical relief once they've done this.

All of this was great. However, when she was told the stitches needed to come out, Harriet freaked out. The doctor asked her what she was so frightened of. 'I told the doctor that without the stitches, I was scared the wound would reopen, the blood would start pumping again and I would lose my hand altogether. I didn't want to be a bleeder.' It was only after this that she remembered the paramedic's words in the ambulance and realised how powerful they had been. We just needed to revisit that movie, ensure it included this important aspect and that Harriet could get distance on this too.

Luckily this doctor had a good bedside manner and took the time to explain how the wound was already showing excellent signs of healing. She also told Harriet how she had seen many wounds much worse than hers which had fully recovered and that this particular medical team had a very good track record. Having reinforced Harriet's confidence in both her healing and the medical team, she then said, 'You need to trust us and your ability to heal.'

'It was a turning point for me,' Harriet said later, 'and when they took the stitches out everything was OK. Because of what she said and because I wasn't a bleeder after all, I began to believe in my body and my future again.' Gradually, she began to regain her confidence that she could make good judgements that would keep her physically safe.

By recognising she had lost confidence, she was also able to recognise its return.

Living by Default

Too many people are living by default, by which I mean that they live with whatever comes their way without really questioning it or taking steps to change those things they don't like about their lives. Living by default means you can come to feel that life, rather than being something to celebrate, is something that you are on the receiving end of.

This was precisely how Lorna felt when she first contacted the Confidence Institute. In the space of less than a month, she had lost an enormous job contract, been dumped by her boyfriend, lost her rented house and been told she was a rubbish mother by a belligerent teenage daughter who had packed up and moved in with her dad. To say Lorna was reeling would be an understatement.

Together we looked at exactly how her life had collapsed on her so spectacularly. At first, Lorna was adamant that everything had happened *to* her. But as we unpicked the events we found that far from being a passive recipient, Lorna had played an active role in the events that had unfolded.

When I pressed her on the loss of her big work contract, she finally admitted she had hated the job and that while she was now terrified she could no longer pay for her lifestyle, secretly she was relieved she no longer had to pretend she liked her work. I asked her why she thought her boyfriend had chosen almost the exact same moment to leave and she admitted she had been questioning his commitment – was it to her or to the lavish lifestyle she had been funding for them both? She explained how she secretly thought it would only be by shedding the money and the lifestyle that she would ever be able to answer that question. As for her daughter's departure, Lorna felt that, like her partner, her daughter had become used to the good life and a mother she could rely on to provide it. Lorna said that with her daughter living under the same roof it had been impossible to think straight, let alone muster the courage to make the changes that were long overdue – including moving to a more affordable house.

Eventually she moved to the country, close to where she had grown up, and found work that paid less but which she enjoyed more than her previous big-bucks job. We continued to work together over the phone. Her relationship with her daughter was improved by them living apart. Last year she married her partner, who had come back to support her and thus proved to her it was not the money or the lifestyle he was invested in but Lorna herself. Things did not turn around for Lorna overnight; it took a year or so for her to really get back on her feet.

As she started to find her way again, Lorna began to keep a journal on her laptop. Each day she would check in with herself. Prior to our final coaching call she emailed me her most recent entry. It's a great description of her journey. Though the content is hers, I think the journey she made is in many ways universal. That's why I asked her if she would be willing to share it with you. She immediately agreed. Here it is:

> I realised I had for years and for far too long been living by default. I didn't like my job, I was worried about my partner's true feelings and I knew my daughter and I had slipped into a pretty abusive relationship but I didn't know what to do to change it all. I had reached the stage where a good day was one where I could call in sick and take a sleeping pill. I had even contemplated suicide, thinking it really was my only way out.
>
> Then, it was as if all these bad things started happening and I kind of forgot I was the person who had wanted things to change in the first place. As I started to remember that, I realised that letting go was a lot less painful than clinging on.

The more life stripped away all the frippery and nonsense, the more I began to see there was something, some kind of essence if you like, that was, that is, irreducibly me. I began to feel more powerful, more positive. Things were still tough but it was as if, through all the trauma, I had begun to find – and like – a more authentic version of me. I realised all the melodrama had not affected this aspect of myself: she was still here. I was intact. I realised too that I was feeling stronger and confident in a different kind of way. I was becoming more optimistic because I now felt more aligned to something more powerful than me, something that I now know I can place my confidence in. And that's inside me.

Why Fear Matters

Fear has a more direct and immediate impact on confidence than any other emotion. (Just ask Harriet.) But extreme fear is not where most of us spend our time. Everyday fear takes a different form and manifests as *avoidance*.

From an NLP viewpoint, fear is just feedback designed to ensure survival. This is true of avoidance too. Avoidance can of course make life easier, but over time it can become very constraining and you could end up missing out on all sorts of things because you lack the confidence to get out and challenge yourself. In other words, you're letting fear win.

In NLP we use fear to elicit more information about an issue. If there's something that's playing on your mind so badly that you're awake at 3 a.m. 'catastrophising' – and 3 a.m., by the way, is when we *all* feel at our most vulnerable, alone and fearful – then allow yourself the catastrophic fantasy, but then ask yourself: *Is this really likely to happen?* If the answer is yes, your next question should be: *And if this happened, what would I do?* Now, instead of tossing and turning for the remainder of the wee small hours, get a pen and paper and write down five things you could do that would make an immediate difference to the nightmare scenario.

From catastrophising to action

Vanessa was losing sleep night after night, scaring herself witless by the thought she was about to lose her job as a flight attendant because of her age and the well-publicised recession-driven cuts. Vanessa had worked herself into such a state that she was no longer eating or sleeping properly and her sister asked if I would talk with her. We talked about the worst case scenario – what would actually happen if she was made redundant – and I then asked Vanessa to write down five things she could do that would make a difference. Here's her list:

1. Register with a recruitment agency now, rather than when the axe falls.
2. Slash my outgoings: I don't need a new sofa. I will make a new budget and stick to it until my future becomes more certain.
3. Speak to my boss and find out the facts; I may be worrying about something that is not going to happen to me.
4. Take stock and review what I really want to do. There are no seventy-year-old cabin crew so I need a different game plan for the future anyway.
5. Ask for support from family and friends while I negotiate my way through this tricky time.

I explained how fear has its own structure, that it requires negative self-talk and a negative visualisation of the future. We talked at length about the importance of acting from a position of strength and authority, which, in Vanessa's case, would mean educating herself on all aspects of redundancy, including her rights, the financial impact and the emotional implications.

Then I asked her to do two things that you've already practised. First to think of people who had bounced back from difficult situations, step into their shoes and learn from them (see page 94). Next I asked her to consider what might be a more positive future emerging from the possible redundancy, then to make a movie of it and finally to step into it and try it on for size.

We can choose our internal dialogue and the movies we run, which, in turn, affect how we respond to those events that challenge our self-belief and our confidence. And we can choose, even when things go wrong, to get something out of an experience and learn from it. Years ago, I was involved in a very difficult negotiation on behalf of a family who were battling it out with their local education authority. After one particularly bruising marathon, my colleague suggested we have a drink to leave it behind. I agreed to the drink but said I wanted to unpack the events of the day. He asked with surprise, 'Haven't you had enough?!' My answer told me a lot about myself, how I learn and how I bounce back. 'Look,' I said, 'if I'm going to feel this bad, I do expect to get something out of it.' It's a mindset I've found incredibly useful – and the best way to ensure I don't make the same mistake again.

Making Confidence a Habit

One of the most effective ways to introduce anything – including confidence – back into our lives is to make a decision to develop it as a regular habit. Here are six simple steps to help you to do this.

1. Become more confident by doing things that require you to be confident.
2. Assume a confident physiology: head up, walk purposefully, breathe fully, look up and out.

3. Make sure the things you introduce that demand more confidence from you are things you can repeat – such as talking to new people each day. Get some practice, then add a new behaviour which is another little stretch.

4. Make sure you have confidence-boosting triggers in your life – including your Confidence Anchor, but also friends and activities that naturally give you that boost.

5. Make sure your triggers are both varied and numerous – restrict your experience and you restrict your confidence.

6. Don't feel like doing something? Do it anyway! Make the investment to build future confidence.

Chapter 9

The Hero's Journey

In Greek mythology, a hero or heroine was originally a demigod. Over time, however, something really important happened: the words hero and heroine came to be used to refer to ordinary mortals who, faced with great difficulty or danger, showed courage. Whether they had to sacrifice what they knew or subjugate their interests and themselves to achieve a greater good, these men and women were heroic because they rose to something that challenged them. These ordinary people were not saints – they had their weaknesses as well as their moments of doubt and fear – but in rising to the challenge they became more than they were before.

You can see all these elements in play in Homer's story of Odysseus' journey home to Ithaca after the Trojan War. On the one hand, *The Odyssey* is the story of our hero's swashbuckling adventures and journey across land and ocean. On the other, it is the story of his inner journey, which means that when he finally returns home, he is not the man who left all those years ago. He really is older and wiser – and more human.

We too go about our business in life physically travelling hither and thither, sometimes local, sometimes far afield. But if that's all we do, we won't have much to show for it. If we're really living, we'll also be making an inner journey that over time changes not only how we see the world but also who we have become.

Having an understanding of your life and what matters to you as a journey gives you a vital tool in becoming more confident: it enables you to take a long view and see things in perspective. Some people are able to take this long view naturally, but more often it is far easier to see the bigger picture in one area of you life, be that work or relationships etc., than in another.

So often we are preoccupied with whatever is right in front of our face. One-off events can highjack us so that we can't see the wood for the trees. Whether these are the cares or the triumphs of the day, the danger is that our state is unduly affected – be it by agony or ecstasy – and our perspective foreshortened. You can apply this way of thinking to so many things. Take relationships: say you have a row with your partner. So is that the end or just a blip along the way? Much of your personal happiness could hang in the balance, depending on your answer. When couples who had been happily married for many years were interviewed about how they'd achieved this, one woman summed up the strategy as 'giving time a chance'. Whatever was happening was seen by her and her husband in a larger context; it was a bigger story than just the drama of the day.[8]

If you think of your life as a journey, what kind of journey has it been so far? And what kind of journey would you like to be on as you go forward over the next few years, say?

To think like this is to think metaphorically – it's the way your unconscious works. It's also the source of creativity. So one of the payoffs of exploring what you're about in this way is that you get to harness a lot of your own unconscious creative energy in a way that brings it into the light of day and puts it at your disposal. That's why in this chapter I'm going to draw on myth and metaphor.

The Power of Metaphor

Sometimes when things are tough you'll hear people say things like: 'My life is full of shit'; 'I'm off my game'; 'I'm drowning in my new job'. These are all metaphors. We use metaphor all the time, but many people often don't realise when they're doing so.

In modern Greek, the word *metaphor* still has a literal, as well as a figurative meaning. In Greek, *meta* means across, with, beside, after; and *pherein* means to carry; while the modern Greek adjective *metaphoroikos* applies to any physical means of transport which carries you from one place to another. In NLP, the term metaphor refers to any 'carrying across of meaning' from one context to another. (Technically, that means it covers both metaphors and similes.)

Why does this matter? Metaphor has the power to let us see things afresh and make sense of them in new ways. A metaphor enables us to look at something and say to ourselves, 'Oh look: this is like that.' Having a metaphor for your journey can be really useful. It can help you make sense of the journey you're on. It can help the brain to make new connections and new neural pathways, which in turn can be like hitting the 'refresh' button on the computer.

It's a remarkable thing, but whenever people want to talk about the really important things in life, they invariably end up talking in metaphors and stories. You want to know how the universe came into being? Well, most cultures will have what's called a creation myth. Right now, the Big Bang could be said to be ours. You want to get to grips with how to live a good life? Every spiritual tradition I know of deals with the big questions by resorting to metaphor in the form of parables and stories. Why? Because stories have a multi-textured richness that engages the conscious and unconscious mind. Every story has multiple meanings and those meanings are ultimately determined by the listener – by you and what the story means to you.

Story-telling is fundamental to being human. Cultural values and taboos are often communicated in myths, fairy stories and teaching tales. Every culture has its own stories that inform its members about what is appropriate and acceptable. The means of dissemination can range from the traditional, like oral story-telling, books and plays, through to newspapers, TV drama and movies. Even the news is a story, really – that's why you'll hear newscasters refer to 'the top story at this hour'.

As far as we know, no human society has ever existed that did not tell itself stories. Stories are endemic and universal, but they are very little understood in our culture. The mistake we often make is to think of story-telling as entertainment. That's only part of – you guessed it – the story. Every team leader, for instance, will have a story, though it may go by a different name, like the business plan.

What people often don't understand is that stories create a coherent narrative that allows us to make sense of our experience – past, present and future. That's why they're so important to us and help give us a sense of identity.

To give people an inspiring vision is a powerful intervention and it means that you're telling them a story. That's why every visionary leader will engage the energies of followers by creating a story that they can engage with. Every story has an effect: it will change the state of the listeners and affect their internal experience. This is true in the boardroom and it's true in a child's bedroom. If you want proof, just watch a child's eyes widen when you say the magic words '*Once upon a time* . . . '! So it makes sense to choose stories with care. If you tell someone a story, you will often have far more effect than if you were to give them some advice or argue a case. Stories can affect how you see yourself and how you feel about yourself and what is possible for you. Stories then can have an impact on your confidence. So it's worth asking:

- What are the stories you've been telling yourself?
- What do they mean for you?
- Do these stories boost your confidence?

Three Key Story-making Processes

The structure and the meaning we give to any particular story will be determined by three processes that have been intensively explored in NLP. These are known as deletion, distortion and generalisation. To see what we're signing up for with any particular story, we would do well to notice what we have decided to delete, generalise or distort. So let's work through these three processes and see how, just by starting to notice them, we can introduce more meaning and more confidence into our lives. All three can work for us or against us. Either way they'll be happening, so it's a smart move to know how to use them to build confidence.

Deletion

Everyone has a history and a personal story, but the truth is this story will have been heavily edited. We have no choice but to delete a lot of our experience; can you imagine how mind-blowing and exhausting it would be if you could remember every single time you have cleaned your teeth in your life and the sequence of events surrounding that one activity? Your brain – and therefore you – would be overwhelmed.

When you start to notice what you are deleting from the stories you run, you will begin to see you always have a choice about what you delete and what you leave in the story of your life. You are, if you like, your own novelist, scriptwriter and cinematographer. Do you delete the good stuff and only notice where you messed up? Do you delete possibilities because that's all they are and you don't think they'll come to anything? How do these choices affect your confidence levels?

You may be choosing to 'look out' through your own eyes or 'look in' on yourself from outside, and again this is a choice that will influence the story you are telling. How does this affect your confidence? Is one way better for you? Try it to find out.

EXERCISE: Your Story

As you begin to analyse and better understand the story you have scripted for yourself and its impact on your confidence levels, answer the following questions:

This is a story about . . . .
The main character (you) is . . . .
The main character changes when . . . .

What do you make of this story? Any script changes needed?

Generalisations

Generalisations can work for good or ill. Sometimes they can create a very black and white view of the world. Remember the client who believed all men were bad news? She proved her point by only choosing men who slotted straight into the character role she had pre-cast for them. On the other hand, we need to make generalisations to make sense of the world and be able to recognise patterns – *oh, this is one of those!* By simply changing the things you are generalising about, you can dramatically change what is going on in your head and, therefore, the script you are running and the way it is affecting your confidence.

Don't believe me? Try this simple exercise on your own or

with a partner. Just write down whatever comes into your head first.

EXERCISE: **Your Generalisations**

Generalisations 1

You never . . . .

You always . . . .

I never . . . .

I always . . . .

Generalisations 2

I must . . . .

You must never . . . .

I have to . . . .

I can't . . . .

There's no way . . . .

Take a look at how you have responded to each of these generalisations. Often people say things like: 'Where did *that* come from?!' But this is the stuff that can be generated out of conscious awareness and can affect your confidence. Sometimes just bringing these thoughts into the light of day is enough to make people laugh and move on.

Now, with regard to each of the statements you made, ask yourself:

- What would happen if you did/didn't?
- What stops you (i.e. the cause)?
- What's in the way?
- What's blocking you?

See which of these questions works best, tweaking them if you need to so that they make sense given your initial statement. This is a really good exercise for triggering new ways of thinking about old stories and for kick-starting your brain into thinking differently about cause and effect. It can help you imagine new possibilities, new characters and new scripts. And that's good for your confidence!

Distortion

You're walking down the street and someone who you don't know looks at you momentarily. You interpret that look as disapproval and start to feel angry and that they have no right, etcetera etcetera. Later you learn that they were lost and too timid to ask you for directions.

Distortion can have a serious impact on the meaning we make of what's happening in our lives! Some people will use distortion as a kind of escape from reality – like Billy Liar in Keith Waterhouse's novel of the same name. It was his only escape from the grim prison of post-war 1950s Britain.

Distortion is all about the meaning we make of our experience. People create meaning that helps or hinders. But most people don't even question the meaning they're making; they act as if their interpretation actually is what's going on.

Next time you decide a particular behaviour 'means' a person is . . . whatever you've decided, ask yourself, how do I know that? What tells me that – and is it true? Ask yourself these questions about other people's behaviour by all means. But equally ask them about your own behaviour. The meaning you've assigned to it – is that helping you become more confident?

* * * * *

A good story is something people remember. What makes it a good story is that it is meaningful to them. That's why a certain novel or movie can really resonate with us at a particular moment in our life. It may even offer us ways to resolve a current dilemma.

The human brain loves to make the links that metaphor allows us to explore. The more metaphor buried in the story for the unconscious mind to unravel, the more satisfying a story will be. We can use stories and metaphors to speak directly to the unconscious mind and allow it to discover and activate its own resources, including those that will support more confident behaviours in both our professional and personal lives. That's why metaphor has been called the dreamwork of language.

Our very sense of who we are – our Identity – comes from the meaning we make of what has happened to us. That meaning is a heavily edited version of the life we've lived. Everybody has a story they tell themselves about who they are, how they've got to where they are, what matters to them and what they want for the future. Sometimes these stories are not very helpful and do not inspire confidence. One client told me: 'I've always been a bit of a failure.' So what kind of story have you been telling yourself? And is it useful?

EXERCISE: The Story of My Life

Pick seven of the most significant events of your life. Write each one down.

When you have all seven, review them and write down beside each one the meaning that event has for you.

As you look at these seven events and what they mean to you, say these words out loud and finish the sentence: *'My life is like . . .'*

Ask yourself: does this metaphor work me? (If not, look again at your seven events and then run *'My life is like . . .'* until you come up with one that does.)

Consider what might happen to this metaphor in the future? Where might it take you? How might it grow and evolve?

If you were to dare to dream, what might your metaphor be for the future? (Feel free to choose something completely different, even off the wall if you wish.)

Ask yourself: what is the story inside me that is waiting to be told? And when am I going to start telling it by living it?

If you want to make a journey, you need to know when is the most auspicious time to do so. This will be partly a function of where you are in yourself – are you ready, for instance? – but it's also about getting your timing right given what's going on in the world. Managing this dynamic tension between inner and outer forces is part of the art of confident living.

> There is a tide in the affairs of men.
> Which, taken at the flood, leads on to fortune;
> Omitted, all the voyage of their life
> Is bound in shallows and in miseries.
> On such a full sea are we now afloat,
> And we must take the current when it serves,
> Or lose our ventures.
>
> *Julius Caesar*, Act IV, Scene 3

When Brutus says these words to Cassius, he is aware that their enemy Octavian is amassing forces that will soon be far greater than they can muster in response. What he's saying is that we need to seize this moment, we need to go with the flow of the tide or we will lose out and never have such an opportunity again. Such moments occur in all our lives. The art is to be aware of them and take action. This is hard to do unless you are in tune with what is going on inside you and what you're about. That's why cultivating that relationship with yourself is so important.

Only then can you have a sense if you're on track. That's where the metaphor of the Hero's Journey comes in.

The Hero's Journey

The concept of the Hero's Journey was introduced to popular thinking by American mythologist Joseph Campbell (1904–87) in his book *The Hero with a Thousand Faces*. Campbell, who spent a lifetime studying the stories and symbols of different religions, cultures and faiths, was interested in what they had in common. He suggested there were a significant number of universal themes including, and especially, the story of the hero who journeys into the unknown and returns transformed. That hero could be described in a thousand ways and take numerous forms – hence the title of his book. But though the particular experiences could vary wildly from culture to culture, there was a common structure underlying the stories because all human beings have similar challenges to face if they are to live a fulfilling life.

These journeys are often described as a series of encounters which occur in the external world. However, their effect is experienced by the person on the inside, too, because the hero is changed by his or her experience. People have argued with Campbell about whether he is correct in his interpretations of some of these myths but that doesn't need to concern us: for our purposes, the best way to understand his contribution is to see it not as anthropology at all but as a literary form that enables us to clarify our own lives.

We need to realise that each of us is the hero of our own journey. The heroic does not have to be astonishing and doesn't need to involve great action. Too many people make themselves small by assuming they're nothing special. They write themselves out of their own script, as it were. They assume only the exceptional person can ever be a hero. In fact, it is the other way round: the ordinary person becomes heroic by doing what is extraordinary for them.

One client was surprised when I talked about what he was dealing with as a call to adventure and change because he didn't think of himself as a hero at all. 'But I feel so scared,' he said. So can a hero be afraid? Of course! If you ever get to see interviews with the guys who were in the 1945 D-Day landings, you realise they were so young (late teens or early twenties) and so scared. But they were inspired by the story they were part of, by their leaders and by the camaraderie of their mates.

There are many versions of the Hero's Journey, each with its own numbered stages. These invariably begin with 'the call' to adventure or change. Then others become involved, be they helpers (guardians) or adversaries (demons). After many trials and tribulations, the journey ends with the return of the hero transformed. I'm going to go with a simple six-stage model that I created and have used with many clients to allow us to put the metaphor to work. As you read through the stages, see what comes to mind for you – where might they apply in your life right now? Maybe you're on the journey and you hadn't even realised. This happens with people sometimes. Or maybe you're getting ready for the next one. In every case, having this outline is like being given a map – it will help you get your bearings.

The Hero's Journey

1. Getting to a place in your life where you are challenged

The old way, which may have been quite comfortable or at least familiar, is no longer viable. Will you cling to it and try to ignore the new realities? Or will you allow your new discomfort to drive you to make new choices and set out again, however hesitantly or even reluctantly, on a journey of learning and discovery?

2. Deciding to accept the challenge

You know you could put it off or try to carry on as normal, but the call is too strong. If you're going to be true to yourself, you need to go in the direction of the unknown. That means you don't quite know what's involved or how to proceed, but you begin anyway.

3. Meeting your helpers (guardians)

Once you commit, you may be surprised at the support that comes your way and also where it comes from. The guardians you will meet are not just those people who will help show you the way, but also those parts of yourself that may now be able to come to life anew and whose drive and determination are going to make all the difference.

4. Meeting and overcoming your temptations (demons)

Again, there may well be external distractions, obstacles, even enemies that you will need to overcome. But they are not just out there in the world. They may also be those parts of yourself you might prefer not to have to face. Face them and you tame them. Tame them by honouring what they are really trying to do for you – then they become your allies.

5. Transforming yourself

It is through this struggle that self-transformation occurs. It's not necessarily easy or comfortable. You will know fear, perhaps even moments of despair because you can't see how things are going to work out and you're not used to being this way. But the payoff is that you get to break out of your old shell and experience a rebirth.

6. Returning home

You're back, but you're in a different place, sometimes physically but certainly inside yourself. You have a clearer sense of yourself and your life purpose. You are the same, but not the same, because your wanderings have given you a new wisdom. Is that it for life? No, but it is the end of one journey. When will your next begin?

The Hero's Journey: the payoff

The Hero's Journey can be lived in the full glare of publicity or be utterly private. Theoretically, you could embark on your own Hero's Journey and nobody but you would ever know anything about it, because in essence the Hero's Journey is not about fame, fortune or recognition from others; it is about living your life on your terms. And here's the best news of all. If you do decide to accept the challenge of your own particular Hero's Journey, I can guarantee you the following outcomes:

- You will defeat your demons and their power will become your power.
- You will conquer your fears and boost your confidence.
- You will change (for the better).

- You will be a better version of the you that you can be.
- You will have a better understanding of your purpose and meaning in the world.
- Your confidence in yourself will soar.

Today, we have hundreds of people who seek celebrity status so that they can feel like they are somebody. This is the complete antithesis of the Hero's Journey; if you do something with your life that has meaning and purpose, you don't need to fill the void in this way. But where there is no Hero's Journey, the heroic impulse gets warped and you end up with a craving for recognition that has no basis in achievement. At best, all you get is your fifteen minutes of fame and a hollow reputation that doesn't last.

If you accept the challenge of the Hero's Journey, you will find yourself challenged somehow, probably more than you have ever been before. However, in addition to finding the stakes raised, you will also have more new possibilities than you ever imagined. You can only understand the meaning of your Journey by embarking on and completing it, and you will discover that those journeys which carry the most meaning of all are, paradoxically, those journeys that are carried out in the service of others.

A Smooth Sea Does Not Make for a Skilled Navigator

Before I ever entered the field of NLP, I originally qualified as a psychotherapist. I remember at the very outset my supervisor telling me: 'I hope you won't be cursed with easy clients to begin with.' Easy clients, he explained, create a false sense of security, even complacency about one's abilities. 'Better to start with difficult clients, who will do far more to improve your skill set,' my supervisor recommended. As it happened, I landed what was to be one of the most difficult clients I ever worked with soon afterwards. My supervisor was right. I learned a lot from working with this client and we worked together, very successfully, for several years. Now I tell this story to my trainee coaches because it will be true for them, too.

In fact, I think that in many walks of life it's when we're challenged that we hone our skills. We now know that understimulation is a fast track to neurological decay. It's back to that simple principle: what you don't use, you lose. So if you want to stay alert and on top of your game, you're going to need to be constantly raising the bar for yourself. The Hero's Journey will do this for you.

But that doesn't mean you've got to do it all on your own. I did not set out into uncharted and rough seas alone; I had a very experienced supervisor to call on, which meant that something that was challenging did not become overwhelming. So who's on your team – on the outside and on the inside?

Meeting the Challenge

The story you are currently telling yourself not only affects the direction you are likely to take in life, but also the very sense you have of yourself. True confidence needs to be deeply rooted in a robust and realistic sense of self-worth and self-esteem. Does your self-story allow this?

The Hero's Journey can provide a structure for ensuring the answer is yes! It may be you can, now that you have a clear definition of it, identify times in your life when you were called on and accepted the challenge to make the Hero's Journey. The path is not necessarily a linear one. Nor is the Journey a one-off life event. If you choose to live fully, you will be called on to make it again and again.

You may, of course, choose not to accept the calling, and that is your prerogative. But if you refuse, you may end up with an uncomfortable feeling that something in your life is not quite right. It's as if you've outgrown your old persona. You can, of course, delay the Journey, but once you take your first step on the path you will discover how just meeting this challenge can begin to address some fundamental questions like:

- What really matters to me?
- How shall I live?
- What do I truly value?

Paradoxically, any new challenge can leave you feeling at the outset less, rather than more, confident in yourself. You may, like Frodo in *The Lord of the Rings*, be willing to accept the challenge but be totally unsure how to achieve the goal. Stepping onto the path of the Hero's Journey will definitely take you outside your comfort zone. But what you will learn is that the confidence you started with was a paltry kind of confidence compared with the belief in yourself, in others and in the value of your life that you will acquire by the end.

Coming Home

The Hero's Journey can only ever be what you make of it. To a greater or lesser extent it will require you to be heroic because when you go beyond what you know you potentially raise the stakes. While this can be exciting it is also very often scary. Invariably when the stakes are raised you will find that what got you this far won't get you much further – you need to do something different. Some people try to stay with the familiar but that's like never leaving home; only when you have the confidence to leave and make the Journey can you contemplate a real homecoming at a later date. Too often people get used to being a certain way and think that is who they are. But consider this,

how you are used to being is not necessarily who you are. The way
you are used to being may, to some degree, just be a habit.

If you are courageous enough to set forth, you will almost certainly take some wrong turns, blunder down blind alleys and
sometimes feel like you're wasting your time. Things may often
not be what they first seemed to be, but that's just par for the
course. Gradually you will become more discriminating and you
will not be fooled so easily in future. Your demons – be they
external obstacles, enemies, temptations or internal struggles
with different aspects of yourself – may seem to spring from
nowhere. But remember: you *can* conquer them, though often
not in the way you might have previously imagined. Frequently
it won't be about defeating them but integrating them in such a
way that, like your internal dialogue, they start to serve you. In
the same way you can expect the unexpected when it comes to
help along the way. Your guardians, be they helpers and well-
wishers, coincidence or serendipity, may well show up when you
least expect them and not take the form you're used to. The trick
is to be open to new gifts in unusual wrapping.

So with all this uncertainty and upheaval why bother to leave
what we presently call home at all? Perhaps the biggest payoff
from the Hero's Journey is that in making it we become more
human and more humane. It is transformative and ultimately
liberating; we find out more of who we are, we grow into being
the best we can be right now and we begin to feel fully *alive*. In
this way too wisdom is born. With it comes a deeper compas-
sion – for both ourselves and for others. There is something very
liberating about coming home at the end of your Journey. You
are more accepting and more inclusive, and you recognise that
all of us – including you – are simply doing our best in any given
circumstance.

At the end of the Hero's Journey you come home, which
simply means you come back to yourself, but you are not the
same as when you started. By accepting the challenge, by finding

the courage to face the unknown, by tackling your demons and finding your guardians, you have transformed yourself.

In Greek mythology Odysseus didn't want to leave home and go to Troy to fight. He even simulated madness to try and avoid his destiny, but to no avail. After years away laying siege to Troy he finally began his homeward journey – only to take years and *years* to get home. His adventures along the way fundamentally changed him so that when he finally did return he was a different man. Whatever your adventures and external achievements, at the end of the day, the journey is ultimately about *you*. You have become the best and most confident version of you that you can be right now. There can be many such journeys in the course of a human life.

The story, like the Journey, goes on for as long as we do.

Chapter 10

Confidence in the Bigger Picture

The way you think of yourself in relation to the larger system you inhabit is very important. You are not an isolated atom, living alone, and you will already have some view of the world and how it works. Whatever you're assuming will be affecting your behaviour in many ways.

It was my friend Robert Dilts who told me this story about Einstein: in the years after the Second World War, a reporter had approached Einstein saying that as he had unlocked the secrets of the atom to such extraordinary effect and given us a new understanding of the universe, he wanted to know what in his view was the most important question facing mankind. Einstein's answer was short and to the point: 'The most important question facing mankind is: is the universe a friendly place?'

The more I've thought about it, the more profound this answer has seemed to me. That universe can be as big or as small as we make it. Whatever its size, what we assume about whether or not it's friendly will affect how we behave, what we imagine is possible in it and what makes sense. (A case in point: when

Transcendental Meditation was introduced into a US prison, the first challenge was to get the inmates even to close their eyes as they sat in the same room for instruction. They were so used to assuming their local environment was anything but friendly that doing this was a major change in itself. To assume you would *not* be attacked was different and liberating – especially when you found you weren't.) So what do you assume? Are you busy defending against all manner of possible attacks? Do you blithely assume everyone wants the best for you? How are you living in your local universe – and do you have a sense of a larger one?

Confidence and Generosity

As you continue on your Journey, you may find it useful to take stock of how your confidence is evolving and developing. By all means use the Confidence Balance Wheel again to see how your scores are changing. But let me suggest another way of checking in with yourself. If you want a useful test of your confidence, you might want to ask yourself: are you becoming more generous in your overall disposition?

One way to measure anyone's confidence is to measure their generosity. In the middle of a recession when your job is uncertain, do you have the same confidence in the future as you did when things seemed secure? Often such uncertainty makes people pull in and withhold out of fear that scarcity is imminent. Real confidence will manifest in generosity, not just materially but in the time, attention and care you are willing to give others.

Having more confidence gives you the freedom to be more generous. Why? Because part of being generous is having the confidence to let go. The more confident you are, the more you can extend yourself to others and to other possible futures, and the less you need to cling to the known. Generosity comes from a sense of abundance, so it makes sense that the two most common obstacles to generosity are scarcity and fearfulness. They don't do a lot for confidence, either.

I am not suggesting you should be generous at your own expense. In fact, to be generous in any way to the wider world, you really need to be generous to yourself. You need to water the root to enjoy the fruit! That is to say, you need to care for yourself if you are to flourish: only then will you have enough to give.

Confidence and Altruism

There's generosity and then there's altruism. Sometimes we'll do something even if it actually is at our expense, because it matters to us enough to make the sacrifice worthwhile. The British writer and journalist Keith Waterhouse once shared this astonishing story, which I have never forgotten.

During the Second World War, with rationing at its height, when food was scarce and working-class families often went hungry, the young Keith walked in from school to find his mother cooking a mouth-watering stew. When he asked for a bowl, his mother said firmly: 'No, this isn't for us. It's for Mrs Brown and her family, down the road.'

Keith protested.

'But I'm really, really hungry,' he wailed.

His mother, exasperated, turned round and smacked him hard.

'You're hungry, they're starving,' she told him.

Sometimes, seeing the bigger picture demands that we go beyond our own immediate concerns because there's something more important that we align with. Even if it's a sacrifice, we know why we're doing what we've chosen to do.

What would that be for you?

Altruism

People often don't recognise their own going-above-and-beyond moments. These can tell you a lot about what really matters to you and what you feel connected to. This can help you get a clearer sense of yourself and what you're really about. And this is very good both for your sense of purpose and your confidence. So try this exercise.

EXERCISE: Getting in Touch with Your Altruism

1. Think of a time when you've gone beyond your comfort zone, when you've really stretched yourself, when you've decided to go above and beyond the call of duty, and where you may even have put yourself in harm's way for another or for a cause.
2. Relive this experience now. Step into it.
3. Why did you do what you did?
4. Why did that matter so much to you?
5. What does this tell you about what is most important to you?
6. What does this tell you about you as a person?

You Are Not Alone

If you want to be more confident and stay that way, then you need to accept that confidence-building is a skill, which, like any other skill, you will need to practise. All skills require repetition and now would be a good time to decide just *how* you plan to practise these new skills. Maintaining the confidence skills you have been building will require an investment in time and attention from you. My suggestion would be to make a commitment to practising little and often.

Building your confidence skills in this way will not only give you a freedom 'from' but a freedom 'to'. You'll be able to experience a freedom from old avoidance behaviours, fearfulness, low self-esteem, or worrying about what others think. On the other side of the equation, there's the freedom to be yourself, to be more loving, to be more spontaneous and creative, to say what you think and to choose how you feel.

Given all this, you may choose to change the company you are keeping. You may also find that some people find your new confidence too threatening. Whatever the reasons, there is a good chance some people around you will change, either in themselves or as players in your life. There are those who suited the 'pre-confident' you. And there are those who will suit the new, more confident you.

One of my clients, who had a lot going for him financially and personally, was in turmoil about where to go next in his life. He decided to take a few days out and went on a short climbing holiday. On the day in question, he was halfway up a rock face when he paused – and that was when it happened. As he looked around, 'I suddenly felt I was in exactly the right place in my life. I didn't understand what I'd do next but it didn't really matter because it would be all right – and I'd be all right.' This feeling and this conviction has stayed with him ever since. He describes this as the single most important experience of his adult life. It has given him a new sense of being alive because, in some way that he doesn't quite understand, he feels he's involved in the unfolding of something that's bigger than just him. This is a man who has no religious affiliations.

You may know people who have had (or you may yourself have had) some kind of experience in which you feel connected to the world/nature/other people in a way that transcends your normal awareness. Sometimes this is accompanied by great feelings of stillness and peace. Other people experience breaking through to a higher level of awareness as a result of personal crisis and pain that shatters their old way of being. Nothing very 'spiritual' about that, you might think, but clients I've worked with have reported it was like shedding an old skin – messy and protracted, but ultimately liberating.

I don't know if you'll have some comparable experience or whether for you it will be in the company of others that you find the changes happening. What I do know is that while this Journey is unique to you, you do not have to make it alone. If you choose, you can make it with others who share your commitment to be more. They may appear in your life quite naturally. But just know that if you want to meet more of them, you only have to come to one of our training events.

You may now be nearing the end of this book, but you are just at the start of your Journey. That's why I want to end by asking you a really important question.

How Big Is Your Big Picture?

People often get stuck in a rut of doing what they do; they forget to look up and see the world around them or the horizon in the distance. Being able to see more than just what's in front of your nose is arguably part of the art of living. So I'm wondering: how do you do this? And indeed: do you do this? If you don't, you're not helping yourself be as confident as you could be and you're more likely to get bogged down in the minutiae of the moment. Of course people have different ways of making sure the trees don't prevent them from seeing the wood. One of the benefits, for instance, of ongoing coaching is that there is an opportunity on some sort of regular basis to step back from the drama of the day and once again take stock and determine what's really important and where you want to be going.

This bigger picture is different for everyone and it's highly personal. It's about what matters to you, what your life is about for you and where you see yourself in the larger scheme of things. Sometimes learning about other people's journeys can help you get your bearings; these can inspire but also map the terrain for us. Personally, I find biographies helpful, not least because you realise just how much goes into achieving what others may assume came easily. Too often people are seduced by stories of easy success and relentless progress. These can actually be debilitating: as one client exclaimed in frustration, 'What's the matter with me? Why isn't my life like that?'

I'm especially drawn to the lives of those who have wanted to create a world that would be better for ordinary people. Part of what I've learnt is that they didn't have it all figured out; they were frequently confused, they stumbled, had highs and lows but they stayed true to what mattered to them. It's as if they could not stop being true to their ideals. I find this inspiring.

I strongly suggest you find what inspires you. But at the same time, don't assume it's only other people who have stories to tell. Don't be afraid to tell your own story – other people may well value hearing about and learning from your experiences. As I'm suggesting you consider telling aspects of your own story, I should probably do so too.

You could say that I'm in the change business. Over the years, I've come to form a view of how change happens and what's needed. I do a lot of demonstrations in my training so that people can see how change really happens. I've often had people who are trainers or presenters from other fields ask me quietly after such a demonstration how I knew that what I was doing was going to work? (Many people mistakenly assume that confidence involves certainty.) The first time this happened, I was completely floored. I really didn't know how to respond, as I couldn't get my head around the question. Actually, I didn't know for sure that what I was doing was going to magically produce the desired result. (And that was the bit they wrongly assumed was the case.) However, I was absolutely confident that whatever happened, I would then be able to respond in a way that would take us forward. That was enough to enable me to be free to explore with the person I was working with how they created their experience and how they could change it in a way that would be better for them.

For me this is an important confidence, both in my own expertise but also in the process that I am part of. Once some advanced students were engaged in a modelling class with me. This is where they get to ask me questions about how I do what I do. One of them said, 'Assuming someone has learnt the techniques you've taught us, what would be your one piece of advice?' It was a great question for me. I'd never thought about it, but I heard myself say, 'My advice would be to *get out of the way* and let the client do what they know how to do – with your help.' Too often people are busy trying to get others to do what they think they should do. It's so much easier if you can support them so that they do it in their own way. Often the way they find to do this is far more creative than anything I could have come up with – and of course it suits them perfectly.

Having coached thousands of people, I have absolute confidence that most people can do what they need to do. All I have to do is create the context in which this is possible and offer tools and means that they can then adapt to make this possible. That makes the particular universe I inhabit, with my trainees and clients, a friendly place where the most amazing things are possible.

In many ways, the art of being happy is being able to create a universe in which you can be yourself and be stretched to be the best of yourself that you can be at this time. For me, this exactly describes what happens when I'm working with people. I don't know what it would be for you, but I would invite you to consider it.

In my case, I couldn't find it out there in the world, so unwittingly I created it by starting my own organisation and creating an environment that I could welcome people into where it is safe to be yourself and to learn. Then to learn how to take this new way of being yourself out into the world so that you can feel free and succeed on your terms by working with others – that's what matters to me. This only really happens when people can come home to themselves, so that's what I'm about. Making it possible for someone to have a sense of what they're really about and to feel comfortable in their own skin. That's the universe I've wanted to create.

For the past twenty years I have been able to both foster this and be nourished by what it brings into being. It's an amazing feeling when students send me accounts of what they're doing with what they learnt. The extraordinary ways in which they're applying what I've taught them, be it in health, business, education, family life, creativity or innovation, frankly dazzle me. And then there are the books they send me as their teacher – which they have written. This tells me I have created a legacy which is not about me but about something much more important – what we may be as human beings. That's what makes me go to bed at the end of the day feeling good.

With true confidence comes true freedom – the freedom to be not just who you really are, but to be as big as you can be. This is not some 'happy clappy' type of feel-good warm bath of emotion. Quite often it involves a real struggle to let go of the familiar and grow into who you could be. Sometimes there are moments when you know you're stepping over such a change threshold on your journey.

Let me tell about one of my thresholds. Maybe it will ring bells for you. International Teaching Seminars – the organisation I'd set up to run training sessions – was flourishing and I wanted to offer the next level of advanced training. I gathered the best trainers from around the world and together we delivered what was a very well-received programme. However, about halfway through I found myself feeling dissatisfied with it. It wasn't the material; it wasn't the trainers. Ultimately I had to face the fact that it was down to me. I'd given myself this safe little role where I'd play second fiddle as the sponsor. Yes, I'd do some of the training, but I thought of the others as the experts. But the time had come when I had to recognise that I was an expert, too, and as long as I didn't rise to the challenge and deliver what I knew this programme could offer, I was selling the people – and my vision and myself – short. I needed to stop playing small and being safe and step up to the plate. The moment of truth came one morning in the shower when I knew that I could either stay small or step up. It was a big moment because I knew that if I did step up, I'd be stepping out too. I would be assuming a mantle for the rest of my professional life that would mean a much more public role and a higher standard to hold myself to in everything I developed thereafter. It was a strange feeling: I felt reluctant, but also as though I had no choice if I was to be true to myself and what matters to me. For a moment the frustration made me slam my heel down hard in the shower – I can still remember the feel-ing – and then it was done. You could say it was like moving from boy to man. I stepped out of that shower a different person. I've been living that mission ever since.

That mission is driven by a larger vision of how people really can have more of what matters to them in their lives. My expe-rience is that we can begin to shape our destiny in keeping with what matters most to us. The clearer I've become about what matters most to me, the easier I have found it to live a fulfilling life. I've found a way to do what matters most to me and to be of service to people in the doing of it. Because I do what I want to see more of in the world, I've been able to do what's most impor-tant to me – and to get paid for it and to support my family in the process. I feel like I am involved in something bigger than me, something that helps me make sense of my experiences, but it is also down to me to keep my feet on the ground, earn a living, pay the mortgage and make sure the people who work with me are properly taken care of. Sometimes people have said to me, 'Oh, it's all right for you to talk – you've got it made. You're established.' What they don't know is that I started as a one-man band with no capital, living in a box room in someone else's house. When I began, people told me I was mad to think, in the words of Benjamin Franklin, that you could 'do well by doing good'.

Certainly you need to offer people something they want in such a way that they can understand what its benefits are for them. But that's part of the art of connecting your vision with the needs of others. These days, much of my work involves helping people work out how to do this so they can begin to create a success pathway that is a true expression of what matters most to them.

Being clear about how you want to live doesn't mean everything will be a smooth ride from then on. Indeed, speaking personally, there have been lots of ups and down over the years. Anyone, for instance, who has run a business knows that you learn to expect the unexpected. All those projected growth charts that depict an ever-upward linear line are pure fiction for 99 per cent of businesses. Neither life nor business is like that. But that's OK. Those downs can certainly be humbling, but they're also important for going to the next level of learning in your own evolution.

Neil Sedaka was incredibly successful as a teen star in the United States until the Beatles arrived. Then overnight the work just dried up. Depressed, he eventually took a big gamble and left the US for the UK, where he was reduced to playing working men's clubs in the North. He described it as 'very humbling'. However, out of that experience came a meeting with 10cc, who produced an album with him and then another. Elton John got to hear about it. He approached Sedaka and ended up recording a number with him, signing him to his new Rocket label and relaunching him in the US, where Elton was now the biggest thing around. Not exactly a straight line of upward and onward. The approximate time frame? Ten years in the wilderness!

Recognising that the Journey is a truly a long and winding road is part of the art of living with confidence. Knowing that you may not understand what the hell is going on or how you've come to be in the place you've arrived at – that, too, is part of the Journey. Not needing to kid yourself you've got it all figured out is part of the art of being confident. The bigger picture is always unfolding and will remain to some extent a mystery.

Being able to live with not knowing while seeking to understand is the mark of a truly confident learner. So let me end for now with my three wishes for you:

- May you not get stuck in your current success.
- May you know that there is more than we can ever comprehend.
- And may you have the confidence to embrace life and let it teach you its lessons.

References

1. Bronson, Po, 'How not to talk to your kids: The inverse power of praise', *New York Magazine*, 19 February 2007

2. Seligman, Martin, *Authentic Happiness: Using the New Positive Psychology to Realise Your Potential for Lasting Fulfilment*, Nicholas Brealey Publishing, 2003

3. Ellis, Albert, *How to Make Yourself Happy and Remarkably Less Disturbed*, Impact Publishers Inc., 1999

4. Kivimaki, Mika, 'Optimism and pessimism as predictors of change in health after death or onset of severe illness in family', *Health Psychology*, Vol 24 (4), pp. 413–421, 2005

5. Aspinwall, L. G. & Staudinger, U. M., 'A psychology of human strengths: Some central issues of an emerging field', in Aspinwall, L. G. & Staudinger, U. M. (eds) *A Psychology of Human Strengths: Fundamental Questions and Future Directions for a Positive Psychology*, American Psychological Association, 2002

6. Stewart, R. et al. 'Dental health, vascular status, and risk of dementia: The Goteborg women's health study', International Society of Vascular Behavioral and Cognitive Disorders meeting, 11–14 July 2007, San Antonio. Final Program. Abstract P-8; Janket, Sok-Ja, 'Poor oral health linked with coronary heart disease', *Journal of the American Dental Association*, Vol 135 (4), p. 416, 2005

7. Gilbert, Daniel, 'What you don't know makes you nervous', *The New York Times* (Opinionator blog, online), 6 May 2010

8. Romney, Ronna and Harrison, Beppie, *Giving Time a Chance: The Secret of a Lasting Marriage*, Bantam Books, 1985

Bibliography

While there are countless books on confidence, the purpose of this short bibliography is to give you some leads should you wish to explore further in a practical way some of the themes we've covered.

Campbell, Joseph, *The Hero with a Thousand Faces*, New World Library, 2008

McDermott, Ian and Jago, Wendy, *The Coaching Bible: The Essential Handbook*, Piatkus, 2005

McDermott, Ian and Shircore, Ian, *Manage Yourself, Manage Your Life: Simple NLP Techniques for Success and Happiness*, Piatkus, 1999

McDermott, Ian and Jago, Wendy, *The NLP Coach: A Comprehensive Guide to Personal Well-being and Professional Success*, Piatkus, 2002

McDermott, Ian and Jago, Wendy, *Your Inner Coach: A Step-by-step Guide to Increasing Personal Fulfilment and Effectivenesss*, 2004

Passmore, Jonathan (ed.) et al, *Excellence in Coaching: The Industry Guide*, Kogan Page Ltd, 2006

Reivich, Karen and Shatté, Andrew, *The Resilience Factor: 7 Keys to Finding Your Inner Strength and Overcoming Life's Hurdles*, Broadway Books, 2003

Romney, Ronna and Harrison, Beppie, *Giving Time a Chance: The Secret of a Lasting Marriage*, Bantam Books, 1985

Seligman, Martin, *Authentic Happiness: Using the New Positive Psychology to Realise Your Potential for Lasting Fulfilment*, Nicholas Brealey Publishing, 2003

Stanley, Thomas and Danko, William, *The Millionaire Next Door: The Surprising Secrets of America's Wealthy*, Simon & Schuster, 2000

Weil, Andrew, *Spontaneous Healing: How to Discover and Enhance Your Body's Natural Ability to Maintain and Heal Itself*, Sphere, 2008

Resources

The Confidence Institute

The purpose of The Confidence Institute is to make it possible for anyone to become more personally and professionally confident. The Institute fulfils its remit by providing practical techniques that can be implemented rapidly and on a step-by-step basis in easily accessible programmes.

The Institute's programmes are available at both elementary and advanced levels. They are supplemented by podcasts and distance-learning packages. In this way the Institute is able to deliver low-cost training both in personal seminars and online to anyone, wherever they may be located.

The Institute also offers in-house professional confidence-building programmes for teams. These focus on specific niche applications, as well as addressing common confidence issues such as making presentations with greater confidence.

Visit: www.confidence-institute.com

International Teaching Seminars (ITS)

International Teaching Seminars has been the home of NLP Coach training for a decade. Delivering practical results, ITS is home to many of the leading figures in the field and is recognised externally by credible third party bodies, such as Henley Business School, as the place to go for training.

If you would like to explore how to make rapid change personally, or explore the health applications of NLP, contact ITS and speak to them about engaging a properly trained NLP Coach.

Or if you are looking for professional training, you can take an NLP Practitioner Training course with ITS to teach you how to maximise your own performance and also learn how to get the best out of others.

International Teaching Seminars is an ISO 9001 certified organisation and has international recognition as an accredited coach training provider from the International Coach Federation (ICF), the largest and most prestigious body overseeing coaching standards in the world.

To learn more about possibilities in coaching and training, visit: www.itsnlp.com or call: +44 (0)1268 777125

Distance Learning

A number of distance-learning CDs are also available. These are provided in collaboration with International Teaching Seminars (ITS). Among these is the Professional Development Programme. This comprehensive 6-CD set and manual focuses on the three crucial dimensions of leadership, managing people and presenting.

More information and resources are available at: www.itsnlp.com

Free Updates

If you would like to receive details of new podcasts and trainings, you can register your interest at: www.confidence-institute.com

Alternatively, you can call: +44 (0)1268 777125

Index

Note: Page numbers in bold refer to diagrams.